Berta
LaFrance

World War I

Mr. Baldwin . . . brings to his task an unusual understanding of a sweeping conflict that seemed to start almost out of casual perversity and to end with a hope for the future. We have long known its bright hope, "the war to end war," was illusory, but it has taken Mr. Baldwin's perspicacity not only as a sound student of military affairs but as a shrewd and impartial observer of geopolitics to put the tragedy into sharp focus.

—N. Y. Times Book Review

Most colorful, gripping and informative.
—Colonel R. Ernest Dupuy

HANSON W. BALDWIN

WORLD WAR I

AN OUTLINE HISTORY

A Black Cat Book

GROVE PRESS, INC.   NEW YORK

CONTENTS

MAPS

FOR MARKIE AND STEVIE AND ANDY
AND BARBIE
AND MY GRANDCHILDREN YET UNBORN:
MAY IT NEVER HAPPEN TO THEM.

ACKNOWLEDGMENTS

To:

Colonels Vincent J. Esposito and G. A. Lincoln, U. S. Military Academy, West Point, N. Y., and their officers for a substantive reading and suggestions.

Mrs. G. S. Lobrano of Chappaqua, N. Y., for helpful suggestions, Chapter I.

To the following authors and publishers for permission to quote passages identified in chapter notes:

The Collected Poems of Rupert Brooke. Reprinted by permission of Dodd, Mead & Company; copyright 1915 by Dodd, Mead & Company; copyright 1943 by Edward Marsh.

Russia Leaves the War by George Kennan, Princeton University Press, 1956.

The Lamps Went Out in Europe by Ludwig Reiners, Pantheon Books, Inc., 1955.

1914 by James Cameron, Holt, Rinehart and Winston, Inc., 1959.

The World Crisis and The Unknown War by Winston S. Churchill, Charles Scribner's Sons, 1927 and 1932.

Military History of the World War by Girard L. McEntee; Charles Scribner's Sons, 1937.

The Great War 1914-1918, by Cyril Falls. Copyright © 1959 by Cyril Falls. Published by G. P. Putnam's Sons, 1959.

A Short Military History of World War I by Colonel Vincent J. Esposito, U.S.A.; U. S. Military Academy, West Point, 1950.

I

THE WAR IN PERSPECTIVE

The cynical Russian proverb, "Eternal peace lasts only until the next year," unfortunately capsules the long and bloody record of man's inhumanity to man. In some 3,457 years of recorded history, there have been more than 3,230 years of war, only 227 years of peace.[1]*

The Great War from 1914 to 1918 was not, therefore, a historical abnormality; it represented, rather, an anticipated and recurrent norm. But in its scope, its violence, and above all, in its totality, it established a precedent. World War I ushered in the century of Total War, of—in the first full sense of the term—global war.

There had been prior epochs in history distinguished by the sanguinary brutality of the combatants, lack of restraint, unlimited means, and absolute aims. "Delenda est Carthago" has been a rallying cry for generations; it has resulted, for many a Carthage, in total annihilation. Attila the Hun knew no mercy, gave no quarter; he left a trail of devastation to mark his conquests. The beleaguered walled towns of the Middle Ages knew their version of Total War; sack, rapine, and death were the penalties for defeat.

Since the days of Thermopylae armies have been decimated or annihilated. The Napoleonic period introduced, in mod-

* Numbers refer to notes, which will be found, arranged by chapters, beginning on page 163.

ern times, the *levée en masse*, or nationwide conscription. And local quarrels have long had global consequences; as Macaulay wrote of Frederick the Great: "In order that he might rob a neighbor whom he had promised to defend, black men fought on the Coromandel, and red men scalped each other by the Great Lakes of North America."

Nor was there anything new about scorched earth or even trench warfare. Sherman blazed a path of ruin to the sea in the dying days of the U.S. Confederacy, and the trenches of Petersburg and Port Arthur (in the Russo-Japanese War) were indices of the increasing firepower of modern armies.

But never before 1914-1918 had a war absorbed so much of the total resources of so many combatants and covered so large a part of the earth. Never had so many nations been involved. Never had the slaughter been so comprehensive and indiscriminate. And never had the participants staked so much for so little.

A Polish banker, I. S. Bloch, was one of the few who forecast (long before the event) the nature and the extent of the conflict:

> . . . war between the great industrial powers is nothing more than mutual suicide. . . . the guns direct thick iron rain. . . . the earth is reddened with blood. . . . there will be increased slaughter . . . increased slaughter on so terrible a scale. . . . Everybody will be entrenched in the next war. It will be a great war of entrenchments. The spade will be as indispensable to a soldier as his rifle. . . . the future of war [is] . . . the bankruptcy of nations and the breakup of the whole social organization. . . .[2]

His words were prophetic. For the Great War of 1914-1918 was the first—but not the last—of the World Wars; it initiated a century, still unfinished, of Totality: Totality of Means; Totality of Ends; Totality of Effort. The phrase "the nation in arms" came to its first full fruition in World War I. The weapons of that war—many of them heralding the developments of World War II—made possible promiscuous, wholesale slaughter, revolutionized tactics. The submarine, the plane, the machine gun, the tank, and poison gas wrote new and foreboding chapters in the history of war. World War I introduced once again an era of Totality, but with a difference; even then, man was beginning to acquire the means—the weapons—capable for the first time in recorded history of destroying man.

The causes of World War I, in Woodrow Wilson's phrase, "run deep into all the obscure soils of history."

They stemmed, too, as all wars do, from the nature of man, and the weakness, pride, venality, and indecisiveness of his leaders.

They stemmed from six hundred years of history, with Germany—fragmented, ever since the mid-thirteenth century, into petty states and princedoms—a parade ground for conquerors. Bismarck, Prince Otto Eduard Leopold von Bismarck-Schönhausen, the Chancellor of "blood and iron," by contrast the so-called "peacemaker" and "peace-keeper" of Europe, was one of the ablest statesman of the nineteenth century. Almost single-handed—aided by an acute sense of timing and rare diplomatic finesse—he enhanced the power of Prussia, and in a series of coups and small wars he transformed the loose-knit, quarreling, ineffective German states into an integrated German empire: the most powerful state in Europe.

But Germany's rise meant French decline. France, hitherto the leading political power on the Continent, was defeated disastrously in a few months of war in 1870-1871. Napoleon III was overthrown, the French monarchy became a republic, and France was obliged to cede Alsace-Lorraine to Germany and pay a huge indemnity. The seeds of lasting bitterness were sown. Irredentism—the war of *revanche*—was forecast. Moltke, the elder, who humbled France in the Franco-Prussian War, warned: "What our sword has won in half a year, our sword must guard for half a century."

Bismarck's political answer to the French spirit of *revanche* was the Triple Alliance: Germany, the Austro-Hungarian empire, and a newly united and independent Italy. Russia, her relations with Austria-Hungary troubled by friction points, was attracted toward France, and the Dual Alliance was formed. Thus, the lines of battle were being drawn, the deadly sides chosen, even before the decline and fall of the Iron Chancellor.

Bismarck, who presided over the birth of modern Germany, fell from power in 1890, soon after Wilhelm II—the Kaiser of World War I—ascended the throne. The tiller of the ship of state was left without a steady hand, and many of the policies which Bismarck had initiated were now pursued to arrogant extravagance with little of the finesse or judgment of the past.

Bismarck had initiated Germany's colonizing career and had started her overseas empire in 1884. But after his fall, the struggle for dominion and riches beyond the seas, and the rapid rise of Germany as a maritime and naval power, posed a threat to the empire upon which "the sun never set" and to the blue-water ascendancy of England. The Entente Cordiale between England and France gradually became the Triple Entente of England, France, and Russia, and the sides were chosen.

Germany's challenge to Britain's supremacy as the world's leading trading and maritime nation and the reaction of Britain and other powers to this economic-military-psychological threat were among the major causes of the First World War. The Kaiser and other leading Germans were greatly influenced by the teachings of Rear Admiral Alfred Thayer Mahan, the great American apostle of sea power. Overseas colonies and overseas trade necessitated merchant and naval shipping, and Britain's centuries-old supremacy at sea was endangered. As German exports surged through the global arteries of trade, protective tariff barriers were erected against this stiff competition in country after country.

Fear and frustration often produce a psychosis of public opinion and threat and counterthreat. Long before 1914, there were Englishmen, like Lord Fisher, the First Sea Lord, who believed that for Britain's safety the German fleet should be "Copenhagened" (destroyed, as Nelson destroyed the Danish fleet at Copenhagen). The Germans, on the other hand, felt, in the Kaiser's words, that they were ringed with bayonets and reacted with what has been called a wave of "foaming chauvinism."

"When it came to argument [conference] Germany invariably laid a revolver upon the table before opening her mouth, and the result was that nations became frightened and coalesced against her."[3]

Espionage and intrigue (the famous Dreyfus case in France in 1893-1898 exposed some of the machinations) further inflamed public opinion.

To these factors must be added another: the decay of the old Europe of kings and emperors. Nationalism and the desire for self-determination flamed brightly long before the cannons spoke in 1914. In Russia, the autocratic rule of the Czar had been repeatedly challenged in attempted revolutions, most of them social, some fanned by ethnic minorities. Turkey, anarchic, autocratic, medieval, maintained the shadow but not the substance of the glories of the sultans of yesterday. The Austro-Hungarian empire, an amalgam of races, was held together only with the pins and patches of compromise and concession, embroidered with the personality of the grand old man of the *ancien régime,* Emperor Franz Josef. The royal kingdom was assailed by minorities, not the least of them the Serbs, who, rallying around Pan-Slavism and encouraged by the support of Russia, looked upon a Greater Serbia, victor in two Balkan wars (1912 against Turkey and 1913 against Bulgaria), as their salvation. In contrast Vienna envisaged expansion of the empire—at Serbia's expense. The Balkans, riven then as now by fierce national animosities and riddled by repeated conflicts, were ominously labeled the "powder keg of Europe." Thus, in a sense, nationalism—German nationalism, stimulated by Bismarck and appealing to the pride of German-speaking peoples everywhere, and Slavic nationalism, as old as the czars —was a major cause of it all.

The advent of modern communications—railroads, the beginning of a road network, and above all the telegraph and the printing press—far from making all men a band of brothers, exacerbated differences, sang the siren song of change.

But if one accepts the fatalistic Tolstoyan theory of history —that men and nations are but marionettes in a drama staged by cosmic forces—then the tragedy of 1914-1918 can now be perceived in retrospect as inevitable. In the half century prior to World War I European population had almost doubled, and armaments expenditures had quintupled. Germany led the pace; her population, by increase and amalgamation, had risen to seventy million, surpassing that of France or Great Britain. Her pig-iron production had exceeded the production of Great Britain by the early 1900's; by 1914 she was exporting more to Great Britain than she was receiving from her, and throughout the world Germany was pressing hard the hitherto invulnerable commercial and banking supremacy of London. A new vigorous and ambitious great power grew to strength in the heart of Europe after 1870, and its challenge to the established order was one of the primary causes of World War I.

"The situation is extraordinary. It is militarism run stark mad," Colonel E. M. House noted in a letter from Berlin to President Woodrow Wilson in May, 1914.[4]

But men are fallible, and it was men—the leaders of both sides—who contributed, with human faults and human virtues, with misplaced strength or shrinking weakness, to debacle.

Germany, which has produced so many brilliant but unbalanced men, was governed by Wilhelm II, a kaiser who "shrank from any thoughts of violence" but trusted his military advisors more than his diplomats, admired power, and spoke with violent bombast, arrogance, vanity, and pride. Unstable, unpredictable, here was a ruler who could slap the Czar of Bulgaria on his behind "in the presence of the entire court," could lie "as naturally as a bird sings," or could recite "between hors d'oeuvres and roast the names of all the Assyrian kings without a hitch and in the correct sequence."[5] The Kaiser's withered arm, injured at birth,

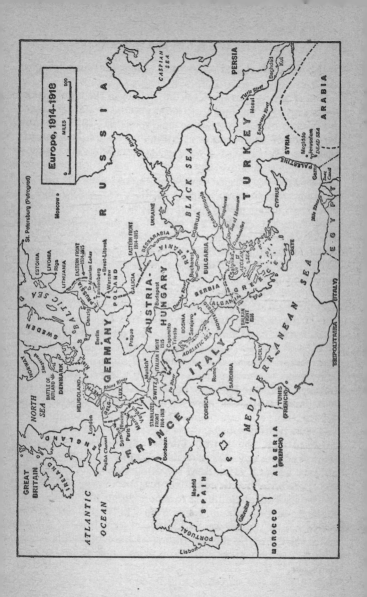

scarred his life psychologically as well as physically. Thus a midwife's slip left its awful mark on history.

Emperor Franz Josef, a machinelike Spartan octogenarian, who slept on an iron cot, bathed in cold water, rose to work at 4:30, galloped across open fields in army maneuvers at the age of eighty, and spoke all the languages of his empire, was a master of hard work and detail but a man with no vision and little emotion.[6]

Italy, newly emerged from division and trying to have its cake and eat it too, was ruled by King Victor Emmanuel III, uncertain either of his crown or his place in history.

Nicholas II of Russia ("Nikky" to the Kaiser), last of the czars, cloaked with the dignity of a beard, a weak, shy, irresolute nature; an emperor who tolerated in his court an evil monk named Rasputin, who, so the people heard, had tried to rape the Czar's young daughter.

In France, Raymond Poincaré, minister of the Right, President of the Republic, native of the lost province of Lorraine, hid an inner uncertainty with an outward rigidity. Of him, and of Aristide Briand, leader of the Left, Georges Clemenceau, who was to come to greatness in the holocaust, once said: "Poincaré knows everything and understands nothing. Briand knows nothing and understands everything."

When Poincaré came to power in 1913, the Belgian ambassador wrote that the new President and his associates "are the inventors and proponents of the nationalistic, militaristic and chauvinistic policy. . . ."

Lord Grey, the British Foreign Secretary—Sir Edward Grey, Viscount of Fallodon—who served two amiable and able masters, Edward VII and his son King George V, was a man who liked nature better than human beings. His quiet diplomacy had made him a foremost figure in the affairs of Europe for a decade, and it was he who forged the Triple Entente. Yet the measure of his greatness must be judged, at least in part, by the magnitude of his failure; his entire edifice went down in dust and ashes on a summer's day of 1914.

Such were the statesmen and leaders of the great powers

of Europe of 1914; some of them distinctive, unusual, in some ways brilliant, but none of them giants of their times.

A host, numbered in the millions, marched to war. The seven European nations, great and small, that entered the lists of battle in late July and early August, 1914, were to increase to thirty countries from every continent before the cease-fire sounded. There were defections and accretions; recruits joined both sides as the war dragged on. Italy at first reneged (holding that her treaty with Germany and Austria-Hungary was defensive, and that Austria-Hungary had started the war); then, in 1915, joined the Allies. The Triple Alliance became the Central Powers, with Germany and Austria-Hungary, the original partners, joined by Turkey and Bulgaria. The Triple Entente—France, Russia, and Great Britain—who drew the sword in defense of tiny Serbia and Belgium, were joined soon or late by the British dominions and colonies beyond the seas, and by Montenegro, Japan, Portugal, Italy, Rumania, Albania, Greece, the United States, Panama, Cuba, Siam (Thailand), Liberia, China, Brazil, Guatemala, Nicaragua, Haiti, Honduras, Costa Rica, the Hejaz, and even tiny San Marino. Bolivia, Ecuador, Peru, and Uruguay broke relations with Germany and were recognized as associated powers. Though the declarations of war by many of these nations, particularly the Latin-American, African, and Asian states, were of far more moral than physical significance, nevertheless, before Armageddon had ended, a local quarrel in the Balkans had engulfed the world, and 65 million men were under arms.

At war's start, six to seven million men faced each other on the tortured terrain of Europe or on the seven seas. Of this number Germany mustered originally about two million (after initial mobilization), to be more than doubled with full mobilization. She was by far the greatest military power in Europe, clearly superior on land to France (which had rebuilt its military strength since 1870) and to Russia, and inferior at sea only to Britain.

The standard tactical unit of all armies, the division, then numbered about 18,000 infantrymen (war's attrition later forced a reduction to 12,000 to 15,000); a horsed cavalry division was about 4,000 to 6,000 men. Germany put into the field at war's start about eighty-seven divisions, increased later to some two hundred. Her army was the best equipped of the time; one German division was reckoned about equal to one and a half or even two Russian and Austro-Hungarian divisions. The Mauser rifle and the Maxim heavy machine gun were standard and highly effective weapons for the infantry. The Germans had a great advantage in medium and heavy artillery. Their horsed cavalrymen—also taught to fight dismounted—still carried saber and lance. "In addition to their unrivalled efficiency in organization and discipline,"[7] the German staff and logistical organization was unexcelled. The use of the railroad to transport and supply armies had been more highly developed in Germany than in any other country. The German tactics and training, though by no means prophetic of what was to come, nevertheless had absorbed the lessons of the Russo-Japanese War (trench systems, importance of artillery, etc.) to a greater degree than other armies.

The Austro-Hungarian Army had few of the assets of its German ally. It mustered at war's start forty-nine divisions totaling 450,000 men (this figure reached 2,700,000 later). Junior officers were competent, and heavy artillery was excellent, in quality "perhaps the best in Europe."[8] But staff work was poor, supply at best indifferent, and there was no national homogeneity to knit men of many different races and tongues into a common whole. "About 75 percent of the officers were of Germanic origin, while only some 25 percent of the soldiers understood German. As the Austrian official history says, 'It often happened that a platoon commander could not make himself intelligible to his motley collection of men.'"[9]

The French Army was second in Europe only to the German. It had *élan* and strong recuperative powers, but it also had weaknesses. The French 75-mm. gun, with a unique recoil system which had been carefully guarded from spies and copyists, was the best of its type in the world, a prototype for modern artillery. But there was little medium or heavy field artillery; about 300 guns to the German 3,500. The cavalry was trained for mounted action only. The officer corps had become embroiled intermittently in politics since the Franco-Prussian War, and the insensate doctrine of *"attaque, attaque, toujours l'attaque"* hobbled imagination and flexibility and—in view of the predominance of the machine gun—represented the wrong doctrine in the wrong place at the wrong time. France mustered some sixty-two divisions initially, 1,650,000 men, later increased to about 3,500,000 men.

The Russian Army's overadvertised "steam roller" had, as its chief asset, "an inexhaustible supply of men . . . hardy, fatalistically brave." Its cavalry was excellent. But it had almost incredible deficiencies in artillery, ammunition, supply and logistics, and its commanders and staff (many of them selected because of social factors) were, with some notable exceptions, incompetent. Even in the middle of the war, in the month of May, 1916, "there were fifteen holidays on which the offices [of the General Staff at Petrograd] were completely closed."[10] The Russians put about 114 divisions—1,400,000 men—in the field at first and subsequently mobilized a peak strength of almost six million men.

The British Army, in contrast to the big conscript armies of the Continent, was a small, well-trained, disciplined professional army, with a high *esprit de corps*. For centuries Britain's military policy had been based upon a political balance of power on the Continent and command of the seas. Her navy was great, her army, though small, had profited greatly from the lessons of the Crimean and Boer wars. Equipment was good, but Britain's major asset on land was the cheerfulness, dependability, and steadiness of "Tommy Atkins." Many of the British officers were competent, but too many were "Colonel Blimps"—the type of brave, devoted, but backward, unimaginative, and dull officer so brilliantly depicted by C. S. Forester, the novelist, in his greatest book, *The General*. Britain could put only seven high-quality divisions—125,000 men—into action initially, but World War I was to force her to depart, to her mortal hurt, from her age-old policy of a small army. Before the war had ended she had drained with conscription the best and the finest, and increased her world-wide strength (including Indian and African troops) to 5,900,000 men.

The smaller armies were outclassed in numbers and equipment, if not always in will to fight, by the military goliaths of Europe. Belgium, with very little communication equipment and a woefully inadequate supply of machine guns and artillery, mustered about 43,000 men at outbreak, increased to 186,000 (seven divisions) after mobilization. Serbia's tough hard-fighting men, fresh from two victorious Balkan wars and accustomed to their native mountains, were organized, after mobilization, in eleven divisions (185,000 men), armed with hand-me-downs and pick-ups. The Bulgarians and the Turks were brave but primitive fighters, many of them (like the Russians) illiterate; essentially armies of foot soldiers, capable of great endurance, amazing triumphs, and ignominious panic.

Such were the armies of Europe on the eve. All of them were essentially horse-drawn armies; motor transport was young. All of them (with the exception of the British professional army) were conscript armies, with large numbers of semitrained reserves, and with ponderous mobilization systems, which required from nine days (in the case of the German Army) to three months (for the Russians) to build up the land forces to full strength. None of them, at war's start, understood that the machine gun was the king of the battlefield.

In the year 1914—only eleven years after the Wright brothers first flew—military aviation was conspicuous by its sparsity. There were only about 500 to 700 military aircraft and some 400 qualified pilots in all of Europe (about 260 of them in France).[11] These were not planes as we now know them, but contraptions of wood and wire with fabric "doped" to the wings. Most of them were single-seater or two-seater biplanes or triplanes, capable of speeds of perhaps sixty to a hundred miles an hour. They were to play a small part in the opening of Armageddon, and were never a decisive factor in World War I. The rigid airship inflated with hydrogen—the Zeppelin—had been developed in Germany to a more advanced state than anywhere else; these cumbersome, vulnerable ships were of limited use in high-seas patrolling and scouting, and, later, in the advent of strategic bombing. Tethered observation balloons were also used.

Britain ruled the seas. The Nelsonian era was gone, never to return, but British predominance in naval power was nevertheless clear. Britain, challenged by increasing German naval power (particularly since 1900), had not been able to maintain fully in new ships her traditional two-power standard (a navy equal or superior to any two-power combination). In dreadnoughts[12]—modern big-gun battleships, with high speeds (21 knots or more)—Britain had twenty ships in 1914, Germany thirteen. But her grand total of all large warships—dreadnoughts, pre-dreadnoughts, battle cruisers, armored cruisers, and cruisers—was 177 to Germany's 87, a preponderance sufficient to make direct fleet-to-fleet challenge on the part of Germany hazardous. Germany, however, had other weapons—the submarine, the torpedo, and the mine—which were to burgeon to deadly bloom as the war advanced. The Russian fleet, in land-locked seas, was a negligible factor, and the Austro-Hungarian fleet, pent up in the Adriatic, was in any case more than overmatched by the French fleet and British men-of-war in the Mediterranean. The war started therefore with an inestimable Allied advantage, command of the seas, a command, however, which had as always to be asserted, fought for, and exercised.

As war came to Europe in 1914 and the stars of the diplomats set, the influence of the generals and the admirals—upon whom was to rest the fate of nations and the course of empires—rose to zenith. They were a mixed lot: strong and weak, inept and able, opportunist and plodder, brilliant and simple.

In Germany, Count Alfred von Schlieffen, author of the strategy intended to win World War I, had completed his great war plan and had retired in 1905. He was succeeded as chief of the general staff by Helmuth von Moltke, nephew of the elder and great von Moltke, but a pale reflection in character and ability of his uncle. He was sixty-six; he "lived and rose on the shadow of a great name . . . and what was worse knew that he was unworthy of it. . . . Moltke lacked confidence in himself in an office chair as well as in the saddle."[13]

The French chief of staff and commander in chief, General (later Marshal) Joseph Jacques Césaire Joffre, was an unlikely looking candidate for military greatness. He was sixty-two when the war started, past his prime, portly and with a big belly, strong physically but slow in thought and decision, placid and calm. He was known as "Papa" Joffre, and some men who misjudged him thought he lacked brains. Nor was he brilliant. But he was not to be bluffed or panicked. He possessed the fighting stamina and perseverance, the determination and common sense, the will to win, without which no commander can achieve greatness. And Joffre achieved greatness; he saved France.

Conrad von Hötzendorff, who served a failing empire, was greater than the Austro-Hungarian Army he controlled. He was a keen strategist; his concepts were sound but his sword was brittle.

The Grand Duke Nicholas, uncle of the Czar, has been variously described as "a strong and able man,"[14] or something of an enigma . . . difficult to rate . . . highly."[15] He, too, wielded a weakened sword, and the efficient management of the enormous, ponderous machine which mobilization started in Russia was beyond him—and perhaps beyond any man.

Field Marshal Sir John French, who commanded the British Expeditionary Force, was a general of very limited ability, but one of his corps commanders, General Sir Douglas Haig, who was to succeed him, had at least two essential military virtues, stubbornness and ruthlessness. Lord Kitchener, first Earl of Khartoum, a symbol of British pride and power, became secretary of state for war and, despite his restricted understanding of logistics, his name and fame and single-mindedness of purpose transformed the British Army from a small professional elite to a tremendous conscript mass.

General Radomir Putnik of Serbia, though ill and restricted to a "superheated room,"[16] knew his Balkans and was a natural genius at the chessboard of war. King Albert of the Belgians, who looked the perfect picture of romantic royalty, was perhaps the best psychological warfare weapon his country possessed; his stalwart resistance and sensitive, melancholy features stirred the hearts of men.

On the seas World War I was no Nelsonian age, although some of the lesser commanders of several navies demonstrated the spirit of a grander time. Vice Admiral (later Admiral) Sir David Beatty, a handsome figure of a man who wore his cap at a rakish tilt, was perhaps the closest physical embodiment of the Nelson tradition: dashing, determined; no student, but a leader. When the war started he commanded the First Battle Cruiser Squadron; later he was to succeed Admiral Sir John Jellicoe, commander in chief of the Grand Fleet. Jellicoe, thorough, sound, cautious, unimaginative, kept firm grasp of the essentials; he knew that upon his shoulders rested the responsibility for British control of the sea; he was the only man, in Winston Churchill's phrase, who "could lose the war in an afternoon." But he lacked flexibility and daring; opportunity knocked at his door in vain.

The Germans had, initially, no naval commander in top position of equal capability. But from January, 1916, on, Admiral Reinhard Scheer, "a real sea dog" known as "Bobschiess" (a gruff, aggressive character) commanded the High Seas Fleet. Vice Admiral Franz von Hipper, "energetic and impulsive . . . with quick perception and a keen 'seaman's eye'" commanded the Scouting Forces.[17] Both were highly capable officers, worthy of their opponents. Hipper was characterized in retrospect as "one of the greatest leaders in naval history,"[18] a somewhat overstated judgment.

The beginning of World War I was different from the start of World War II. The ponderous mobilization processes of the great conscript armies meant that time was needed before any nation could muster its full strength; even the beginning of mobilization—which could not possibly be concealed—telegraphed the punch and indicated that the die for war was cast.

It had been building up, this war that few men wanted, more and more rapidly ever since 1900. There had been crisis after crisis: in Morocco in 1905 (where the colonial ambitions of France and Germany clashed); in the Slav-Serb provinces of Bosnia and Herzegovina in 1908 (then annexed by Austria, thus infuriating Serbia and Russia); again in the Agadir incident in Morocco in 1911 (in which Germany tried gunboat diplomacy, but was forced to back down after a fiery speech by David Lloyd George, a brilliant, unstable Welshman, then British chancellor of the exchequer). By the beginning of that fateful summer of 1914, Colonel Edward M. House, who was President Wilson's confidant and advisor, declared: "It only needs a spark to set the whole thing off."

Gavrilo Princip, a half-demented, consumptive eighteen-year-old, drunk on the deadliest brew of all, fanatic nationalism, provided the spark. The Archduke Francis Ferdinand, nephew of Emperor Franz Josef of Austria-Hungary and heir to the throne, in June, 1914, paid his first visit to Bosnia since that province had been annexed. He was accompanied by his morganatic wife, despite the fact that he had been warned there was danger of a demonstration against him by the Serbian population of the province.

The archduke's official reception in Sarajevo, capital of Bosnia—then little known save to students and travelers—occurred on June 28. He was greeted by bombs. Seven assassins, hired by the Serbian "Black Hand" (the president was a colonel of the Serbian general staff, Dragutin Dimitrijevich, known as Apis, "foremost European specialist in political murder"[19]), lined the route. The first assassin failed. A bomb rolled off the folded top of the archduke's automobile, wounded some bystanders. Five of the assassins fled, one was arrested; Princip remained. With a Browning pistol, given to him by the chief of intelligence section of the Serbian general staff,[20] he fired the shots heard round the world.

Princip killed both the archduke, heir apparent to the Austrian throne, and his consort; his accomplices immediately sent a telegram to Belgrade: EXCELLENT SALE OF BOTH HORSES.[21]

Princip set the spark to the "powder keg of the Balkans." The assassination provided an opportunity to Vienna to humble Serbia. But Russia was a friend of the Slavic Serbs. Count Leopold von Berchtold, the Austrian foreign minister, and General Conrad von Hötzendorff, chief of staff, played their cards carefully. An emissary was sent to Berlin to secure Germany's backing. On July 5, 1914, the Kaiser, in Winston Churchill's words, gave Vienna a "blank check, valid against the whole resources of the German Empire, to fill out at pleasure. . . ." He provided assurances of complete support and then blithely sailed away to Norway on his yacht, shrugging off the responsibilities of state during the three weeks of crisis that followed.

There was still hope for peace—for the world did not know then that the die was cast by the Kaiser's casual support. Even so, it was not until mid-July that the aging Emperor Franz Josef voted for war with Serbia with two words: *"Dann ja."*

There followed a stiff ultimatum, accepted with but minor reservations by Serbia on July 25, but the hour had already struck; the day of Armageddon had dawned and the Four Horsemen were not to be denied. Serbia mobilized; the ponderous machinery of war went clanking into gear all across Europe; Germany urged her Austro-Hungarian ally to strike quickly and to present the world with a *fait accompli*.

There was now no turning back; neither mediation nor localization of the conflict was any longer possible. Men and events joined the fatal ranks of history to march, face forward, to inexorable doom. On July 28, Austria declared war on Serbia; one day later shells were falling in Belgrade. Russia commenced general mobilization on July 30; Germany sent an ultimatum to Russia; then one to France.

On August 1, Germany declared war on Russia, and during that same night German troops violated Luxembourg to seize the railways needed for troop transport and supply in the West. Germany declared war on France on August 3, and on the morning of August 4, after a prior ultimatum, she informed Belgium that for "security" purposes German troops would move into the little country. King Albert appealed for aid and Britain, which had jointly agreed with Germany, France, Austria, Hungary, and Russia to respect Belgium neutrality, sought assurances that the guarantee would be fulfilled. The German Chancellor Moritz von Bethmann-Hollweg, "an amiable but anemic personality,"[22] merely expressed astonishment that London would go to war for a "scrap of paper," and at midnight, August 4, 1914, Britain joined the spreading conflict.

In the Prime Minister's room in the House of Commons, Mr. [Herbert Henry] Asquith was sitting alone when his wife Margot entered.

She said, "So, it's all up?"

He answered without looking up, "Yes, it's all up."

. . . "I got up and leaned my head against his," she said, "and we could not speak for tears."[23]

And so the cataclysm started, and in the words of Viscount Grey of Fallodon, whose days of glory had ended, "The lamps are going out all over Europe; we shall not see them lit again in our lifetime."

II

THE DIE IS CAST—1914

IN THE FIVE CLOSING MONTHS of 1914 the marching armies
reaped Europe's grapes of wrath. From that lush August,
which marked the end of an epoch, through a chill December, the untried warriors grappled, bled, and died. Two
great battles—decisive to the course of the war, the fate of
nations, and the future of history—were fought in West and
East. Serbia repelled invasion. Japan and Turkey joined the
spreading conflict and in the mists of the North Sea and deep
in southern latitudes the navies dueled with voice of thunder,
tongue of flame.

THE WESTERN FRONT

Graf Alfred von Schlieffen died at eighty, less than two
years before the Great War started. But his spirit led the
armies of Germany in the opening gambits in the West. His
last words epitomized the German strategy in August and
September, 1914.

"It must come to a fight. Only make the right wing strong,"
he is reputed to have said.

The Schlieffen plan, formulated by and named for
von Schlieffen, who was Helmuth von Moltke's predeces-
sor as chief of the Great General Staff, contemplated a
two-front war. It envisaged at the war's start concentration

of the maximum possible German strength and all of the best troops in the West, with the Eastern Front facing the slowly mobilizing Russians held by relatively small reserve forces. On the Western Front a powerful German offensive, keyed to a right flank or Western envelopment of the French armies, was to lead, it was hoped, to encirclement and destruction of those armies and quick victory. Schlieffen felt that direct attack across the German border against the French system of fortifications from Belfort to Verdun (which he regarded as "almost impregnable") could yield little substantive result. His plan, then, was keyed to a great wheel through Belgium and the southeastern part of Holland, thus outflanking (as in World War II) the French fortifications. The "strong right wing" of the German armies would "pursue the enemy relentlessly" in a series of successive outflanking movements, then would sweep like a scythe west and south of Paris, entrapping the French armies and annihilating them against their own fortifications and the Swiss border.[1]

Schlieffen understood that the French doctrine of war was wed to the *offensive à outrance;* he expected a French assault on the southeastern flank (the German left flank) in Alsace-Lorraine, but he recognized that any French advance there would simply facilitate the great scythelike sweep of his right wing and the envelopment of the French left.

This plan, one of the most famous battle scenarios of history, was modified before the war's beginning by Von Moltke.[2] Indeed, many critics believe that these modifications doomed the German strategy even before the guns spoke. Moltke eliminated the invasion of Holland, thus forcing his two right-wing armies through the fortified bottleneck of Liége. Worried about the possible eruption of French troops on German soil on his left, he reduced the strength of the right wing to strengthen his left. And similarly worried about the weak German forces earmarked for the Eastern Front, opposite the Russians, he milked away more than four and a half corps from the Western Front's right wing to bolster the East.

Thus, the Great War started in the West, with both of

the principal armies committed to the offensive.

The forces were almost evenly matched in numbers: there were seventy-eight German divisions opposed by sixty-two French, seven Belgian and (originally) four British divisions.[3]

The two right-wing German armies—the First (Alexander von Kluck) and the Second (Karl von Bülow)—had to break through the fortified Belgian area of Liége; quick reduction of the forts and the early establishment of bridgeheads across the Meuse were vital to a German victory. Twelve obsolescent forts manned by 40,000 men ringed Liége, and their defense was entrusted to General Gérard Leman, who had taught the theories of war for twenty-five years at the Belgian War College. The studies of a lifetime and the handwritten exhortation of his sovereign, King Albert—"I charge you to hold to the end . . . the position which you have been entrusted to defend"—were no proof against 17-inch Skoda howitzers. The attack on the forts began on the night of August 5-6 and, aided in considerable part by the drive and daring of General Erich Ludendorff, a staff officer of the Second Army, whose name was to be known to fame, all was over by August 16. General Leman, faithful to the end, was pulled unconscious but alive from the wreckage. The German blitz had started.

The ensuing series of battles, which extended from Belgium to Alsace-Lorraine, have come to be known collectively as the Battle of the Frontiers. They were but brief and indecisive actions, but the clash of the great armies—totaling almost 3,500,000 men—cost thousands of casualties. In Alsace-Lorraine, from Mülhausen near the Swiss frontier to south of Metz, the French, in a short-lived advance, penetrated slowly from August 14 to 20 into their "lost provinces." But Prince Rupprecht, with the Sixth and Seventh German armies, counterattacked and drove the French back. Although the Germans missed a major victory, Moltke, importuned and misled by the ambitious and energetic optimism of Prince Rupprecht's chief of staff, mistook the shadow for the substance. Instead of strengthening the right wing in accordance with the Schlieffen plan, Moltke supported the partial German successes on his left and authorized continued futile attacks which lasted until September 9-10 against the French fortifications in this area.

On the Belgian flank, the German armies had marched through Brussels on August 20 and penetrated the dense forest country of the Ardennes. Joffre had planned a major offensive in this area, so Frenchman and German came face to face in a general engagement neither expected on August 22. Again, the Germans tasted the heady wine of victory, and the French forces, after a two-day sanguinary struggle, commenced a general retreat which was not to end until the Marne.

Meanwhile, the German First and Second armies (Kluck and Bülow), the tip of the wide-swinging scythe, continued their great sweep through Belgium. King Albert's forlorn indomitables, with Liége lost and Namur encircled, had fallen back into fortified Antwerp and were out of the main fight. Joffre did not fully recognize the danger to his western flank (he had not believed the Germans had men enough for the wide sweep of the Schlieffen plan) until about August 21. Bülow, swinging wide across the Sambre River, came into head-on collision with Charles Lanrezac's Fifth French Army, tired by ninety miles of marching in August heat. Farther west, the First German Army smashed into a defensive position at Mons held by 30,000 British of the newly landed British Expeditionary Force, under Field Marshal Sir John French. The resultant battles of the Sambre and Mons ended once again in German successes and in general Allied withdrawal. By late August the Battle of the Frontiers had ended; all the long-held hopes of a massive French offensive were smashed and the dead and dying littered the battlefields. Yet the Germans were feeling the strain, and Moltke had failed to keep the right wing strong.

The campaign was now fast approaching climax with troops of both sides drooping with weariness and literally falling asleep in the saddle. Kluck and Bülow pushed the pursuit, and Kluck's First Army crashed headlong once again into one British corps at Le Cateau on August 26. Both sides lost heavily and the British sacrificed thirty-eight guns to cover their retreat. Three days later at Guise, Lanrezac's Fifth French army launched an indecisive assault, supposedly against the flank of Kluck's First Army, but actually against elements of Bülow's Second Army. Guise had two results. It eased the pressure on the retiring British and the French Sixth and Fourth armies on their flanks, thus giving Joffre time—the most precious commodity in war. And it produced its own hero named Franchet d'Esperey, a corps commander, whose star was now in the ascendancy.

In late August and early September, "Papa" Joffre, stern and unforgiving in France's hour of need, relieved or shifted dozens of generals who had been tried and found wanting. Two army commanders were among them, including Lanrezac, indecisive and weak, whose command of the Fifth Army had led to British mistrust and recriminations. Franchet d'Esperey relieved him on September 3.

By late August Joffre had begun to move his chessmen. The build-up of a Sixth French Army, composed of reservists and of troops shifted from Alsace-Lorraine to the western flank had well started, and the so-called Foch Detachment, later to become the Ninth Army, commanded by Ferdinand Foch, had been established (August 29) to bolster the right flank of the hard-pressed Fifth Army. Joffre was turning Paris, under Joseph Gallieni, an old colonial hero and its military governor, into an armed camp and was heavily strengthening his western (left) flank. Before the end of the Marne battle, seven corps had been added to the French forces on the vital western flank.

Meanwhile Moltke had done little more than compound his errors. Worried by the alarmist reports of his commander in East Prussia, he had pulled two more corps away from his sweeping scythe (August 25) and started them toward the Russian front. Cyril Falls calls this "one of the fatal decisions of the war."[4] The three right flank (western) German armies —the First, Second and Third—had detached and left behind sizable forces to contain the Belgian Army in Antwerp and to besiege fortified Namur, Maubeuge, and Givet. By

August 26 the right wing had been reduced from sixteen to eleven corps.

Thus, the French achieved a vital local superiority on the western flank of about 1.8 to one.[5]

Kluck, aggressive but rash and bullheaded, reached the Marne on September 2, and soon pushed spearheads across it. That same night Moltke, now convinced that his right-wing armies were not strong enough to swing around Paris, ordered the tip of the scythe to wheel north and east of the city. The Germans were tired from forced marches and continuous fighting, and supplies and replacements had failed, in many instances, to keep pace with the battle. Moltke, in contrast to Joffre, did not really have control of his troops and he was still living in something of a fool's paradise. His headquarters in Luxembourg were far behind the front, and radio, still in its technological infancy, was uncertain and inadequate. The commercial telephone lines had been torn up by the German cavalry; couriers were the principal link between GHQ and the fighting—and they lagged far behind events.

The new French Sixth Army (Michel Joseph Maunoury commanding) hastily concentrated in the entrenched camp of Paris. The French capital was evacuated by the government on September 2 and grizzled Gallieni, the military governor, was left in command. He made some grandiose and stirring pronouncements and pushed work on the surrounding fortifications. On September 4, after reconnaissance reports indicated the German First Army was pushing southward across the Marne, Gallieni ordered the Sixth Army to move to meet the Germans.

Joffre's plan for his massive counterattack, which he had started to prepare as early as August 25, gave the Sixth Army a key role. It was to march north along the Marne and cross the Ourcq River on September 6 to attack the German right wing in the flank. On the same day other French armies were to attack for one hundred miles along the front as far east as Verdun. Joffre was staking everything on "one turn of pitch and toss."

But military operations rarely are carried out according to plan, and on September 5, instead of September 6, elements of Maunoury's army blundered into one of Kluck's corps in an action neither side anticipated. It sparked the Battle of the Marne upon which the fate of France depended.

Immediately the battle roared to furious crescendo all along the front. The Sixth Army, heavily engaged on September 7 and 8 against Kluck's First Army, was reinforced with two regiments of infantry, sent from Paris by taxicab —"the first movement of troops to a battlefield by motor transport."[6]

A gap between Kluck's First and Bülow's Second armies, which had been opened as the German right wing swung toward Paris (partially because of Kluck's insubordinate interpretation of orders), was exploited, though slowly, by the British, and by the French Fifth Army under its new aggressive commander, later to become a marshal of France, Franchet d'Esperey. D'Esperey, after futile daylight assaults, crossed the Petit-Morin River in a surprise night attack on September 8-9, seized Marchais-en-Brie, and forced Bülow to withdraw and bend back his right flank, opening still further the gap between the First and Second armies. It was a turning point. At the same time Ferdinand Foch's new Ninth Army, which had been echeloned into the front to the east of the Fifth, was heavily attacked by elements of two German armies, driving south in answer to Moltke's revised plan. It was on the eighth—the critical day in the Battle of the Marne—that Foch is supposed to have sent his famous dispatch to Joffre:

> Hard pressed on my right. My center is yielding. Impossible to maneuver. Situation excellent. I attack.[7]

The French were in deep trouble; in fact, on many parts of the battlefield, they were all but beaten—but did not know it. The government was in Bordeaux and some German troops could see the tip of the Eiffel Tower on the horizon. But Joffre, carefully controlling his battle, was calm to the point of phlegmatism; Moltke, hours behind the fight, was nervous and uncertain. By the eighth, Moltke, who had given his army commanders almost carte blanche, became alarmed, largely because of an intercepted radio message, by the gap between Bülow's Second and Kluck's First armies. He sent Lieutenant Colonel Richard Hentsch, chief of the intelligence section at GHQ, by automobile to the right-wing armies to find out what was going on.

Hentsch, a staff officer, carried with him the full authority of GHQ, but buttressed only by somewhat equivocal verbal instructions. He sent back reports after brief visits to the Fifth, Fourth, and Third German armies, and then—on the critical day of September 8—he visited Bülow's Second Army headquarters, where, according to some interpretations, he found Bülow "personally defeated."[8] Before Hentsch left for the First Army early on the ninth, Bülow, with Hentsch's acquiescence, had planned retreat behind the Marne and then behind the Vesle.

Bülow's planned retreat and the gap between the First and Second armies would leave Kluck isolated and in danger of envelopment. He was still attacking on the ninth against the flank of the French Sixth Army and the assault was progressing well, but Kluck's flank was in the air. Hentsch explained Bülow's intended movements to Kluck's Chief of Staff, and advised, suggested, or ordered (the exact responsibility and sequence of events is in doubt) a retreat.

The "miracle of the Marne" had occurred—in large part because Joffre possessed (in the words of Voltaire's description of Marlborough) "that calm courage in the midst of tumult, that security of soul in danger, which the English call a cool head."

The German retreat was general; their armies fell back behind the Aisne on a line from Noyon to Verdun. Moltke, panicky, reported to the Kaiser:

"Your Majesty, we have lost the war!"[9]

He was superseded, secretly, by Erich von Falkenhayn, but he was right; the war was lost to Germany—though it required four more years of bloodletting to prove it.

The Marne was a decisive strategic and moral victory for

France and it presaged the end of the war of movement on the Western Front and the beginning of trench stalemate.

There ensued, in the closing months of 1914, a series of battles which was to extend the front from Switzerland to the sea.

The Allies, following up the German retreat, attacked the enemy line in the First Battle of the Aisne—the first taste of trench warfare. The offensive was virtually ended on September 18, though fighting continued with negligible gains for another ten days. Then, in a sequence of bloody engagements, each side tried, in succession, to outflank the other in what has become known as the "Race to the Sea."

King Albert, with his field army, evacuated besieged Antwerp on October 6 and the town fell on the ninth. Falkenhayn, with his young volunteers advancing, singing, to their deaths, tried to penetrate the lightly held Allied line in the First Battle of Ypres in the low-lying Flanders plain. British troops, moved to the flank from the center of the line, and Belgian troops plus French reserves, aided by floods and inundations, barely stemmed the assault and mounted a futile counteroffensive in a month (October 12 to November 11) of bloody fighting.

Ypres, with its mud and blood and horror, was the final large battle in the West in 1914. Both sides—gasping and spent from months of furious and unrelenting combat—dug trenches, strung barbed wire, prepared fixed positions, which were not to vary for the next three years by more than ten miles in either direction. The machine gun reigned supreme.

Nineteen-fourteen, in the West, ended with the Germans in control of the richest part of France. The professional cadres of all armies, who had led the march to war, were all but wiped out. The French had suffered far more than half a million casualties. Tommy Atkins, the regular soldier of the British Expeditionary Force, had been virtually eliminated by Ypres and the preceding battles; the Belgians had lost most of their country, and perhaps 40 percent of their field army. But Germany had paid a heavy price, and she had lost the war. Nineteen-fourteen sowed the dragon's teeth on the

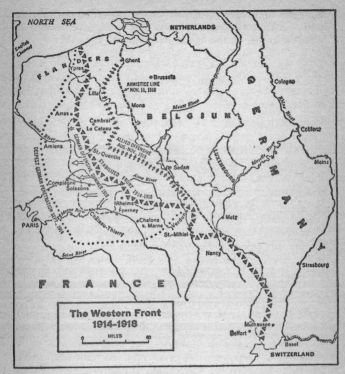

The Western Front
1914-1918

Western Front; the harvest of the Four Horsemen in the years to come was to be whole generations of Europe's youth and pride.

THE EASTERN FRONT

In its scale, in its slaughter, in the exertions of the combatants, in its military kaleidoscope, it far surpasses by magnitude and intensity all similar human episodes. . . . Hard and sombre war; war of winter; bleak and barren regions; long marches forward and back again under heavy burdens; horses dying in the traces; wounded frozen in their own blood;

the dead uncounted, unburied; living pressed again into the mill. . . . Here all Central Europe tore itself to pieces and expired in agony, to rise again, unrecognizable. . . .[10]

Only the pen of a Winston Churchill could thus do justice to the vast space, the severity of hardship, and the redundancy of horror that the Eastern Front presented throughout the war. Someone has said, as Colonel G. L. McEntee has noted, that in the West the armies were too big for the front; in the East the front was too big for the armies.

Here, in the forests and the lakes and the watercourses, another decisive battle was fought in the East in the closing months of 1914, while the fate of nations was being staked in the West upon the chessboard of the Marne.

Russia, true to her prewar staff promises to her allies, and in answer to the urgent requests of France during August, launched an attack upon Germany and Austria before her own mobilization had been completed.

The salient of Russian Poland dominated strategy. The bulk of the ready Russian forces—thirty-eight and a half divisions, organized in four armies—faced an equal number of Austro-Hungarian divisions along the southern flank and eastern shoulder of the salient. Two Russian armies—seventeen and a half divisions, organized in two armies—drove into East Prussia from the northern flank and northeastern shoulder of the salient. They were opposed by a single German army—the Eighth, fourteen divisions strong. The Russians had the advantage in numbers, but in skill, training, weapons, and equipment (particularly communications equipment), in road and rail network, and, as events showed, in generalship, the Central Powers were far superior.

The German forces, unlike the Russian, were tightly controlled, a control based on excellent intelligence of the enemy's movements and capabilities, and even of his intentions—knowledge gained, in particular, from interception of Russian messages, and, to a lesser extent, from air reconnaissance.

The Russians launched their offensive on August 13, even

though only one-third of their strength had been mobilized, and supply and supporting units were conspicuous by their absence.

The drive into East Prussia thrust two spearheads against the Eighth Army: one by the First Russian Army (Pavel Rennenkampf, commanding), north of the Masurian Lakes, a chain of fortified lakes approximately across the middle of East Prussia; another by the Second Russian Army (Aleksandr Samsonov), south of the lakes. Both were supposed to be coordinated by the Army Group Commander, General Y. G. Zhilinski, but inadequate signal equipment, poor staff work, lack of vehicles, and poor generalship made coordination a quality of the East Prussian invasion that was notably lacking.

Years before, Von Schlieffen had anticipated just such an attack. The Germans planned to meet it by concentrating first against the First Army, then, by utilizing their interior, or central, position and their excellent communications networks, to shuttle their forces to the west against the Second Army.

Nevertheless, the drive netted an initial success, which had for the Russians an unfortunate result. Lieutenant General Max von Prittwitz-Graffron, an egocentric political general, commanded the German Eighth Army. He was a man of outer arrogance but inner weakness. After a first contact with Rennenkampf at Stallupönen, on August 17, an action forced by General Hermann François, an able and aggressive German corps commander, three German corps of the Eighth Army made a poorly coordinated attack on the First Russian Army at Gumbinnen on August 20 on the same day that Samsonov's army, far to the south, crossed the East Prussian frontier. One corps scored a tactical success at Gumbinnen; the other two were repulsed, and Prittwitz faltered.[11] He called Moltke at GHQ in the West, and told him he intended to retire behind the Vistula River, thus surrendering all of East Prussia. This was enough for Moltke. Prittwitz had to go. His successor was General Paul von Hindenburg, called from retirement, a "wooden Titan" who in another era was to play figurehead to a man named Adolf Hitler. Named as

Hindenburg's chief of staff was Erich Ludendorff, who had already helped to take the Liége forts.

But before they arrived, events were moving to climax. Lieutenant Colonel Max Hoffmann, operations officer on the Eighth Army staff, demonstrated to Prittwitz that retreat across the Vistula was almost certainly impossible until Samsonov's army had been repulsed. Accordingly Prittwitz approved Hoffmann's brilliant plan for moving by railroad and forced marches the bulk of the Eighth Army from Gumbinnen and the Insterburg gap about 130 miles to the south and west to concentrate against Samsonov. One German cavalry division—supported by the fortress troops of Königsberg behind their battlements—was left behind to check the entire Russian First Army.

The redeployment, which took from August 21-25, was well started when Hindenburg and Ludendorff assumed command on the night of August 23. The XX German Corps, which had been blocking the slow Samsonov advance, was already in action; two others, spurred by Ludendorff, were hurled against Samsonov's right flank on the twenty-sixth. On the twenty-seventh another corps—General François' I—reached the Russian left flank and started an encircling attack.

The resulting Battle of Tannenberg, which was virtually ended by August 30, was a modern Cannae. Both of Samsonov's flanks were turned; his center crushed and encircled. In some five to six days of fighting, the Russian Second Army was destroyed. Perhaps a third of its strength escaped; the rest—125,000 prisoners, thousands of dead[12]—bore witness to the first great German victory in the East, a victory paid for at the cost of about 13,000 casualties, dead, wounded, and missing. Samsonov disappeared; he died, most historians believe, by his own hand. His last words were reputed to be: "The Czar trusted me."

Meanwhile, in the North, Rennenkampf's First Army continued its plodding advance in blissful ignorance, until too late, of the catastrophe to the south.

When at length news of the Tannenberg disaster reached Rennenkampf he halted his advance; "refused" or withdrew his south flank behind the Masurian Lakes and prepared to give battle. It took Hindenburg, Ludendorff, and Max Hoffmann just four days to redeploy the Eighth Army and to plan the new battle. The Germans planned to fix the First Army by frontal attacks and to turn the southern flank by penetrating gaps in the chain of lakes.

Rennenkampf committed virtually his entire force to a static, linear defense, keeping only two divisions in reserve —thus sacrificing flexibility. Yet, initially, his troops fought well.

Four German corps, including two that had arrived from the Western Front on September 2 (too late for Tannenberg but at a time when the crucial Battle of the Marne was approaching its climax), launched a fixing frontal attack on September 9. But a system of deep trenches nullified the German superiority in heavy artillery, and the attack was repulsed. The success was short-lived. Before dawn on the same day the German I Corps, which had marched some seventy-seven miles in four days driven by its swashbuckling general, Von François, who had played a stellar role at Tannenberg, struck Rennenkampf's southern flank and rolled it up in utter confusion. But Rennenkampf, despite his earlier sluggishness, reacted rapidly and correctly; he ordered a general retirement and covered it with a strong two-division counterattack on September 10. Another Tannenberg eluded Hindenburg; nevertheless, the First Battle of the Masurian Lakes expelled the last of the Russian forces from East Prussian soil and bagged another great haul of Russian prisoners. The fighting petered out in rear-guard actions by September 17, and a classic campaign was ended.

Like the Battle of the Marne in the West, the Tannenberg-Masurian Lakes campaign had tremendous consequences. It did not free Germany from the strategic shackles of a two-front war, and its results were partially cancelled by the concurrent Russian victories in Austrian Galicia. Nevertheless, its military, strategic, political, and psychological shock waves were felt throughout the world. Two Russian armies were broken, with a total loss of perhaps 300,000 men. The myth of the so-called Russian "steam roller" was exposed; indeed, instead of confronting the enemy with an inexorable force the Russians plodded blindly to their doom, their mistakes and misjudgments so many and so crass as to become material for any war college case book.

Tannenberg was a defeat so devastating some historians feel that the Russians "suffered a blow from which they never fully recovered and which contributed in no small measure to their later elimination from the war."[13] This seems an overstatement, for the Russians, as two great wars have demonstrated, have a capacity to absorb terrible casualties and great defeats. The battle nevertheless influenced the campaigns in East and West; if Germany (ultimately) lost the war when she lost the Battle of the Marne, she prolonged it at Tannenberg. For the Germans, indeed, the news of Tannenberg helped to obscure the news of the Marne. In Hindenburg and Ludendorff, the German people had found hero images which they were to follow to Götterdämmerung.

Defeated disastrously in East Prussia, the Russians were, nevertheless, scoring successes farther to the south. On the southern flank of the Polish salient and down to the Rumanian frontier, four Russian armies—the Fourth, Fifth, Third, and Eighth—under General Nikolai Ivanov, faced three Austrian armies—the First, Fourth, Third and part of the Second, Conrad von Hötzendorff commanding—along a 200-mile Galician front. (The Austrian Fifth and Sixth armies and the bulk of the Second Army had been deployed against Serbia.)

Conrad took the offensive on August 23, trying to beat the Russian mobilization schedule. His main effort was on his left (western flank) between the Vistula and the Bug rivers toward Lublin and Kholm. The Russian plan was almost the exact counterpart of Conrad's; as a result the two giants met in head-on collision. In the battles of Krasnik (August 23-26) and Komarov (August 26-31), the strong Austrian left wing —the First and Fourth armies—almost won a great victory. But both contestants were something like blindfolded prize fighters; each knew little of the other's movements, and confused orders and poor coordination denied Conrad more than a tactical success.

Meanwhile the weak Austrian right (southeastern flank)— the Third Army, bolstered by other detachments—was in trouble. The Russian Third and Eighth armies in the battle of the Gnila Lipa River (August 26 to 30), outnumbering the Austrians at least threefold, overpowered the Third Army and forced it back, with heavy casualties, many miles to the west of Lemberg (its starting point). The Russian left wing was now in position to move against the flank and rear of the First and Fourth Austrian armies.

Conrad, reinforced by the rest of his Second Army, hurriedly shifted north from the Serbian front, attempted in the Battle of Rava-Russkaya (September 6 to 10) to reorient and redeploy his forces and outflank the Russian Third and Eighth armies. Both sides attacked in confused and indecisive fighting. But the Austrian redeployment left a forty-mile gap between the First Austrian Army on the left flank and the rest of Conrad's battle line. Russian cavalry exploited this gap and imperiled the Austrian rear. The Fourth Austrian Army got the warning in time—not from its own cavalry patrols, but from uncoded enemy radio messages, sent in the "clear." On September 11, Conrad ordered a retirement behind the San River; then on September 16, to the Gorlice-Tarnow line, with his left flank resting on the Vistula, his right on the Carpathians, 135 miles west of (behind) Lemberg where the bright hopes and brave dreams of Austrian victory had started.

Conrad's retreat left in Russian hands all of Austrian Galicia, except for the beleaguered fortress of Przemysl— surrounded, miles behind the front, by the high tide of the Russian advance.

The Galician battles cost the Austrians about 250,000 dead and wounded, and 100,000 prisoners out of less than one million participating troops—a huge toll. It was once again the handwriting on the wall of history—the beginning of the agonized end of an empire which had served its purpose.

The Russian victories imperiled the rich province of

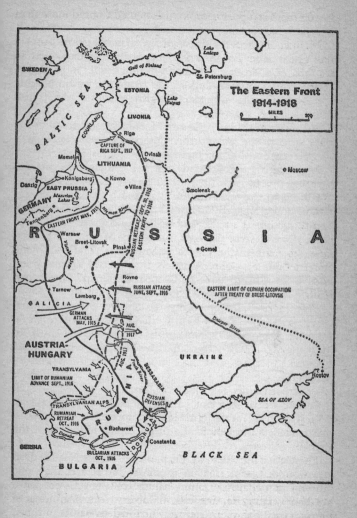

The Eastern Front
1914-1918

MILES
0   200

German Silesia, and the successful triumvirate, Hindenburg-
Ludendorff-Hoffmann, moved with four of their corps from
East Prussia to meet the threat. Once again the Germans used
with remarkable Teutonic efficiency their excellent railroad
network. The troops were shifted about 500 miles to the
Cracow area in eleven days in the latter part of September
in some 750 trains—a model of logistic planning and execution.[14]

These relatively small German forces, reconstituted (with
other units) as the Ninth Army, launched an audacious spoiling offensive into Poland on September 28, just as the Grand
Duke Nicholas, the Russian supreme commander, was re-
deploying his forces with the aid of strong reinforcements.
The Austrians covered the German south flank astride the
Vistula and advanced up to the San River. The German
thrust had initial success and made rapid progress; by October 12, the Germans were in sight of Warsaw. But, like
Paris, its somber spires were unattainable. The weight of
Russian numbers—approximately four armies to one, sixty
Russian divisions to eighteen German—told, and after fierce
fighting along the Vistula the Germans gave up all their
gains and retired, in good order, to their frontier, hampering
the enemy's follow-up by blown bridges, scorched earth, and
extensive demolitions. The Austrians recoiled, too, back
from the San, once again and for the last time leaving
Przemysl to its fate, and the campaign of southwest Poland
was over.

It had been a game of bloody tit-for-tat; it had delayed and
distracted, but it had not halted the Russian preparations
for a Silesian offensive. Hindenburg, appointed commander
in chief of all German forces on the Eastern Front on November 1, faced greatly superior enemy forces—the Ninth
Army against the Russian Fifth, Fourth, and Ninth. The
Austrians were shattered; in the north Russian forces were
moving again across the thinly held borders of East Prussia.

Rich Silesia, with its war-essential industries and mines, was
again imperiled; evacuation and dismantlement began.

But again the Germans invoked their strategic mobility.

keyed to the railroad, and commenced another bold spoiling offensive. They were aided by intercepted Russian radio messages, a factor which helped the Germans on the Eastern Front throughout the war. The Ninth Army, now under August von Mackensen, who had been a corps commander in East Prussia, was concentrated between Thorn and Posen in early November, and was launched on November 11, with part of the Eighth Army from East Prussia, against the flank of the projected Russian advance into Silesia.

The drive almost yielded another Tannenberg, and then, by turnabout led to encirclement of a German corps and an epic battle at Lodz. Mackensen's offensive smashed at least fifty miles by mid-November, and exploited a gap between the Russian First and Second armies. But Grand Duke Nicholas acted with decision, moved the Fifth Army up from the south and formed a counterattack force. The envelopers became enveloped. The German XXV Reserve Corps at Lodz fought a confused and epic battle against much larger enemy forces, and finally broke out in late November, complete with prisoners and captured guns. By December 6, as the Russians pulled back and established a new and solid line, the Germans moved into Lodz, but the major fighting was over.

The two lightning moves in southwest and northwest Poland, though reverses, or at best, drawn battles tactically, had smashed the planned Russian Silesian offensive, and indeed relieved for the duration of the war the threat to Germany proper.

By now, a stream of reinforcements from the Western Front and newly mobilized units commenced to bolster Hindenburg's strength; by the end of 1914—in the bitter cold of winter—the Eastern Front was quiet.

This huge tidal ebb and flow—seemingly dispassionate, inexorable, pointless—left the aftermath of its bloodletting upon the rest of the war. The army of the Austro-Hungarian empire lost in the battles in Galicia most of its well-trained regular officers—the only cement which had held together the amalgam of multilingual races. The Russians, too, suffered heavily; their regular officers died in hundreds among the windrows of the slain.

SERBIA

Conrad initially had deployed three armies against Serbia, including the Second, which was eventually shifted to the Russian front. The shift gave the Serbs, who had mobilized half a million men (backed by some 40,000 to 50,000 militia of tiny Montenegro), an initial slight numerical as well as a qualitative advantage, and ensured for the Austrians a hot reception.[15] The first Austrian invasion, across the Sava and Drina rivers, ground to a standstill in the stark Serbian mountains, and recoiled again across the frontiers—all in the space of twelve days (August 12-24), and at the cost of about 50,000 men. In early September, the Austrians tried again, got across the rivers, and managed to hold two small bridgeheads but bogged down in trench stalemate.

Two months later, the Austrians, humiliated by the defeats and checkmates inflicted upon their empire by a small nation of less than five million people, made a determined attempt to finish the business. They now outnumbered the Serbians about three to two in fighting men and were far superior in quality and quantity of equipment and ammunition. After seesaw stubborn fighting in the terrible rigors of a mountain winter, the Austrians outflanked Belgrade, and occupied the Serbian capital on December 2. But the wily Serbian commander Putnik was awaiting the arrival of ammunition (the Serbs suffered a perpetual shortage). He launched a counter-offensive on December 3, and by the ninth the Austrians were once again in full retreat—the only monuments to their conquests the rutted, trampled mud, the flotsam of a retreating army, the bodies by the wayside, the gouts of blood upon the snow. . . . By December 16, Belgrade was reoccupied and the enemy expelled, but at high cost for a few months of triumph: perhaps one hundred thousand Serbs, dead, wounded, or prisoners, and a similar number of Austrians.

TURKEY

The German General Liman von Sanders commenced to train and reorganize the Turkish Army in late 1913, and in early August of 1914, as war was coming to Europe, Turkey signed a secret agreement with Germany. But it took German wooing, British psychological blunders, and some months of war to bring the "sick man of Europe" into the conflict.

Soon after the war started, two German cruisers, the *Goeben* and the *Breslau,* which had been cruising in the Mediterranean, escaped to the sanctuary of a Turkish port and became "Turkish" in name. A Turkish fleet under German command shelled the Russian port of Odessa on October 30, and the act put Turkey, *de facto,* into the spreading conflict. (*De jure,* her declaration of war was October 31.)

Her entry automatically created new theaters of war and new problems as well as new opportunities. The Dardanelles-Black Sea supply route to Russia was closed, but the Turkish empire in Asia, weak from the dry rot of centuries, was now vulnerable to attack. The Turkish fronts were characterized by great distances, extremes of climate—from the frigid cold of the Caucasus to the heat of the desert—and poor communications. There were no through rail routes, and it required weeks of arduous travel to reach Baghdad from Constantinople. The Turks mustered initially about forty divisions, almost half a million men, eventually organized in four armies: the First in European Turkey; the Second in Asia Minor; the Third on the Russian frontier near the Caucasus; the Fourth along the Levant coast from Palestine to Sinai, and two corps in Mesopotamia. Small campaigns immediately started in Mesopotamia near the head of the Persian Gulf, where the British raj drew power from India, and along the Suez Canal which Britain defended from her Egyptian fief. Major elements of a British Indian division seized Basra (November 22) and advanced to the junction of the Tigris and Euphrates in Mesopotamia. And an omen of what was to come was a showy but futile bombardment of the Turkish Dardanelles forts in November by elements of the British fleet.

By far the most important battle in the Turkish theater was the bitter winter struggle in November, December, and early January, 1915, on the Caucasus front at altitudes as high as 8,000 feet. The egocentric, incompetent Enver Pasha, Turkish minister of war, took personal command of the Third Army of about 150,000 men. He was opposed by about one hundred thousand Russians. The Turks, guided by Enver Pasha's dreams of glory, planned to strike first, but the Russians anticipated them. Near Kars and Ardahan the hapless Turks suffered a heavy defeat. A major part of the Third Army disappeared—dead in battle or from freezing cold. By early January, the climactic date, an entire Turkish corps had been annihilated.

OUTLYING THEATERS

Japan, whose sun had been rising over the Pacific ever since the Russo-Japanese War, avidly joined the Allies on August 22; her principal war aims were the hope of territorial booty and prestige. She had much to gain and little to lose. Her initial objectives were the German outposts and Pacific colonies, particularly Tsingtao in China, to which the Japanese, aided by the British, promptly laid siege. Tsingtao surrendered on November 7. The Japanese also occupied the undefended Caroline and Marshall islands. Japanese men-of-war cruised the Pacific trade routes, aiding the British to scour the seas clean of German shipping.

In South Africa, a short-lived Boer revolt was suppressed.

The German colonies in Africa, the first gems in the Kaiser's imperial diadem of empire, immediately felt the backwash of conflict. Togoland was conquered by British forces before the end of August, and British and French moved into the Cameroons. But in November, German East Africa repulsed an expeditionary force convoyed from India, and mixed white-native forces under the over-all command of a minor military genius, Lieutenant Colonel (later General)

Paul von Lettow-Vorbeck, staged short-lived invasions of British East Africa during 1914.

THE WAR AT SEA

The influence of sea power upon history was felt from the war's beginning. Those "far-distant, storm-beaten ships" of the British Grand Fleet, upon which (to paraphrase Alfred Thayer Mahan) the Kaiser never looked, stood between him and the dominion of the world. From the start of hostilities, the power of the naval blockade—slow, at first incomplete, but gradually increasing—tightened inexorably about the Central Powers like the coils of a python.

The application to Germany of this crunching force was immensely aided by Britain's geographical position—that fortunate accident of nature which had had so much to do in past history with English greatness. The British Isles lie squarely athwart the western face of Europe and enclose and interdict the North Sea and the maritime approaches to Germany and the Baltic.

German shipping, except for a few blockade runners and raiders, was scoured from the seas, and by the end of 1914 the pattern of German trade had completely altered. The flow of overseas commerce to and from the adjoining neutrals —Holland, Denmark, Norway, Sweden—was swollen with goods ultimately destined for Germany; direct German overseas trade became minuscule.

The British Grand Fleet, superior in strength to the German High Sea Fleet in a ratio of perhaps three to two, was the ultimate power behind the blockade. To gain control of the sea—free use of the sea lanes for their own purpose and denial of this use to Britain—the Germans had either to defeat the Grand Fleet decisively enough to eliminate its margin of superiority or to whittle away, by attrition or by a *guerre de course* (a kind of maritime guerrilla warfare), the sinews of British sea power. The second course of action became the fundamental German naval strategy—a strategy frequently adopted in history by a weaker naval power. The

High Seas Fleet was used, particularly after Admiral Scheer took command in 1916, in raids and forays in the North Sea area and in opportunistic attempts to catch the Grand Fleet or elements of it at a disadvantage. But even if the High Seas Fleet had not undertaken such forays, it still possessed at anchor the value of a "fleet in being." Britain had to retain the bulk of her naval power in the North Sea area on watch and ward to check and block and counter any German attempt at breakout into the North Atlantic and to foil attacks upon the troop convoys and supply lines to England and France.

The strength of the High Seas Fleet was great enough to prevent a close blockade of the German coast but, concealed by the mists of the North Sea, the Grand Fleet was the principal keystone of a distant blockade, with cruisers and light forces steaming across the latitudes and longitudes of the world actually carrying out the pedestrian work of chivvying the German flag from the world's oceans.

In much of World War I, the fleets fought "blind" by modern standards. There was no radar, and but few aircraft. The Germans used Zeppelins for scouting for the High Seas Fleet, but, particularly for the British, the best source of information was communications intelligence—interception of enemy radio messages and radio direction finding. Scouting and patrolling by destroyers, cruisers, and submarines provided the tactical information essential to a commander. Gun laying was visual. The Germans used stereopticon range finders, the British chiefly coincidence types. Fire rarely was opened at more than 16,000 to 18,000 yards. German ships, subdivided into many watertight compartments, had developed the science of damage control to a greater extent than the British. Technically, tactically, the Germans were, ship-for-ship, superior to the British, but they had fewer ships, and they operated under an essentially defensive doctrine.

Thus for these two opposing fleets, among the greatest in world history, much of the war was spent in weary and watchful waiting—the British from the cold dreary bases at Scapa

Flow in the Orkneys, and Cromarty in Scotland, the Germans at Bremerhaven and Wilhelmshaven in the Jade (with older ships based at Kiel in the Baltic) behind the guns of the fortified island of Heligoland and the mine fields of Heligoland Bight.

The British won an initial clash. Vice Admiral Sir David Beatty, cocky and aggressive, led his battle cruisers into Heligoland Bight to beard the enemy in his lair. The Germans, with methodical precision, covered their returning destroyer patrols each dawn with a force of light cruisers. Unvarying routine, no matter how desirable in some professions or in personal life, can be a source of weakness in war. Routine cost the Germans on August 28 three light cruisers and a destroyer as their light forces were surprised in the dawn mists by Beatty's heavy guns.[16]

The sinking of the *Köln, Mainz,* and *Ariadne* and of the destroyer V-187, and shell hits on five other light craft, cost the Germans 712 men killed, 149 wounded, and 381 prisoners, among them the first flag officer of any navy killed in the war. The British lost thirty-two killed and others wounded in three ships, one of them heavily damaged.

On August 27, the day before the Heligoland battle, the German light cruiser *Magdeburg* was lost in the Baltic after stranding on a rocky bottom in a dense fog. The *Magdeburg's* codes, ciphers, and signal books were recovered by the Russians and transmitted to Britain. Incredibly, the Germans did not change their codes and ciphers for some months. Decoded radio messages played a major role in the battles to come.

A portent of things to come was soon evident. On September 22, the old armored cruisers *Aboukir, Cressy,* and *Hogue* were sunk in less than an hour off the coast of Holland by a single German submarine, the U-9.

The *Aboukir* took it first, and quickly turned on her side and sank. Her sisters stopped dead in the water, lowered their boats, and lay to, to help the struggling survivors. The U-9 potted them one after the other like sitting ducks, and 1,400 English seamen died. Such behavior may have been, like the charge of the Light Brigade at Balaklava, gallant, but it was not war; orders were issued prohibiting major ships to stop for the survivors of torpedoed ones.

There quickly followed other losses to submarines and mines. British cruiser *Hawke* went down off Scotland (five hundred dead), torpedoed by a German U-boat on October 15, and British dreadnought *Audacious* sank off Ireland on the twenty-seventh, victim of a submarine-laid mine.

On October 20, the U-17 wrote history a short distance off the Norwegian coast. For the first time in the war a submarine stopped and sank a merchant vessel, the British steamer *Glitra*.

In an unprecedented move, the British declared the entire North Sea as of November 5, a controlled military area, which neutral ships entered at their peril. The move, though it induced friction with the United States, greatly facilitated the British blockade.

In mid-December, elements of the High Seas Fleet bombarded Hartlepool and Scarborough on a foray to the English coast, killing 120 civilians and wounding 400. The raid caused the British to detach some forces from the Grand Fleet to provide coast defense (which was one of its purposes).

But the real drama of the naval war at sea in 1914 was played out far from the coasts of England. On the far-flung trade routes, the chase had started. Scattered around the world when the war commenced were five armed merchant raiders, flying the imperial flag of Germany; the cruisers *Königsberg, Karlsruhe, Dresden, Leipsig, Nürnberg,* and *Emden,* and a squadron under Admiral Graf Spee—its most important ships, the armored cruisers *Scharnhorst* and *Gneisenau* (11,000 tons displacement; eight 8.2-inch guns; six 6-inch).

Königsberg sank the British cruiser *Pegasus* at Zanzibar (September 20) and was then blockaded upriver in German East Africa to form an important part of the German defenses in what became an epic little campaign. *Karlsruhe* went marauding in the Atlantic with heavy damage to Allied trade and blew up, 300 miles off Barbados, hoist by her own petard, apparently an accidental explosion in her magazines. *Emden,* most famous of the German raiders, cut a wide swath of destruction across the trade routes of the Indian Ocean to die in flaming ruin on a tropic reef of the Cocos Islands on November 9 under the guns of the Australian cruiser *Sydney.*

That left Spee five cruisers (plus the auxiliary cruisers or armed merchant ships which operated independently). Spee stood across the Pacific from Tsingtao, China, and won, off Coronel, Chile, one of the most lopsided actions in naval history.

Scharnhorst, Gneisenau, Leipsig, and *Nürnberg* met at sunset (November 1) a scratch and hastily formed British squadron commanded by Rear Admiral Sir Christopher G. F. M. Cradock. The British armored cruisers *Good Hope* and *Monmouth,* with the light cruiser *Glasgow* and auxiliary cruiser *Otranto* (armed merchantman) were part of the British forces searching for Spee and his cruisers. Cradock's flagship, the *Good Hope,* was the largest ship in either squadron (14,100 tons) and she mounted the biggest guns (two 9.2-inch; one forward, one aft; and sixteen 6-inch and fourteen 3-inch amidships). *Monmouth* was smaller (9,800 tons with fourteen 6-inch guns and eight 3-inch). Light cruiser *Glasgow* was outclassed, and *Otranto,* an auxiliary cruiser, was merely a good target. Cradock had left behind him an old, slow, coast-defense ship, the *Canopus,* armed with four 12-inch guns. Her guns could sink the German squadron if they ventured within range, but her wheezing engines could not catch Spee's ships. So Cradock left her behind; what would have happened had she been at Coronel belongs to the "ifs" of history.

The slaughter did not last long. The British ships were stronger on paper than in fact. They were old and were manned chiefly by reservists; the Germans had crack crews. Spee put his ships hull down against the dark loom of the land; Cradock was silhouetted against the sunset's afterglow; the British gunners were firing blind. The sea was up; the ships wallowed in the troughs or took it green over the bows as the fight raged. It was a Viking's end for Cradock and his two largest ships; *Good Hope,* afire, staggered out of the fight, and a huge explosion which sent a sheet of flame two hundred feet into the air heralded her end. *Monmouth* died later, on fire, steam escaping from her gashed hull, listed so heavily to port she could not return the fire of *Nürnberg.* But she did not strike; she capsized in the heavy sea; "to the last her flags were flying and still flew as she went down."[17] *Glasgow* took five bad hits but she and *Otranto* fled to fight another day. The British lost two ships with Cradock and all the men aboard—1,654 seamen. Spee had two men wounded.

But bad beginning, brighter end. The lion—challenged on his own hearth, the endless reaches of the sea—was aroused. The Admiralty detached two battle cruisers from the Grand Fleet, concentrated ships from many squadrons on the trade routes, particularly in the South Atlantic.

Spee rounded the Horn; made the mistake, against the divided advice of his captains, of touching at the Falkland Islands to coal and to harry the British flag. At 7:30 A.M. on December 8, his light cruisers sighted tripod masts in Port Stanley; Vice Admiral Sir Doveton Sturdee with battle cruisers *Invincible* and *Inflexible* (17,250 tons; eight 12-inch guns) had arrived the day before. Sturdee and his battle cruisers with seven other lesser men-of-war were as surprised as Spee. The British were coaling or repairing ship, unready for action; again the pen of history paused. Even Corbett admits that Sturdee at anchor and without steam "had been caught at a disadvantage and the prospects should the Germans press home an attack without delay were far from pleasant."[18]

But Spee thought only of escape, and escape, with a whole long day for the chase, was not to be. British stokers sweated in the firerooms; the ships raised steam. The British battle cruisers, "black with coal dust and in coaling rig," stood out to sea in jig time, and easily overtook the Germans. The battle opened at 12:50 P.M.; at 1:20 Spee saw the handwriting on the wall and ordered his light cruisers to scatter and fend for themselves. But it was too late. The battle was another slaughter. The Germans this time were outranged, outgunned, outrun, outnumbered. *Scharnhorst* sank—a shambles, at 4:17 P.M.; *Gneisenau* at 6 P.M., *Nürnberg* was run down at 7:29; *Leipsig* at 9 P.M. in the full dark. *Nürnberg's* survivors, dying in the icy water, were attacked by giant albatrosses. Only little *Dresden* escaped, to be sunk three months later off Valparaiso, Chile. The British saved some two hundred survivors, but many Germans drowned in freezing agony. British losses were slight despite many shell hits; armor saved the English tars.

In the Mediterranean, the French drew first blood. They sank the Austrian light cruiser *Zenta* (August 16) off the Dalmatian coast. But Austrian submarines damaged the French dreadnought *Jean Bart* (December 21).

As 1914 ended, thousands of men, spiderlike, were spinning tangled strands of barbed wire along a 350-mile front from Switzerland to the sea. The Western Front was bogged down in trench warfare. In the East, along a 1,150-mile front, where the deep bitter cold of winter held the land in frozen grip, the tired gladiators, worn and gasping, bided their time. The war's first great battles had ended; victory had been denied, reputations smashed. Air power had played a very limited role, but its reconnaissance reports had aided the groping giants on the ground, and—significantly—just before Christmas German seaplanes had dropped the first bombs on England.

The war had spread around the world; patterns of trade and finance, social contacts and personal friendships were disrupted. Christmas in the trenches, on the bleak plains of Poland, and in the foothills of the Carpathians brought a little easement of enmity; there was even fraternization and exchange of simple gifts between enemies. But it was not to last. The bitter seeds had been sown; the flowers of evil were bound to bloom. The mills of propaganda already were grinding exceeding fine. The Allies had lost more than a million and a half casualties in five months—an unprecedented toll of blood; the losses of the Central Powers cannot have been much less.

Europe was locked in a death grip.

III

THE GIANTS ARE LOCKED—1915

THE YOUNG MEN still queued before the recruiting stations in certainty of purpose and with high resolve. Death might beckon, but if the sacrifice brought the brave new world it would not be in vain. It was an era in which Rupert Brooke could write:

> If I should die, think only this of me:
> That there's some corner of a foreign field
> That is for ever England.

Nineteen-fifteen broadened the war. The British almost, but not quite, changed its course in the Dardanelles campaign. Italy and Bulgaria entered the lists. Serbia died. The *Lusitania* was sunk. The Russians recoiled; the Western Front was deadlocked. Poison gas, the Zeppelin, and the submarine added to holocaust.

THE EASTERN FRONT

Falkenhayn was a "Western Fronter"; that is, he believed victory could only be won in the West and he still clung to the mirage of a breakthrough. But Hindenburg and Ludendorff identified victory with the strategy they espoused—attack in the East.

The Kaiser decided the dispute in mid-January. Four

newly mobilized German corps were to reinforce the Eastern Front and Hindenburg and Conrad were to launch converging offensives from East Prussia and the Carpathians.

The initial Austrian offensive spearheaded by the Third and Fourth armies, stiffened by a largely German southern army, made few gains (except in the extreme south) and on March 18, the besieged fortress of Przemysl surrendered to the Russians with one hundred thousand men and hundreds of guns.

But, as always when the Germans bore the brunt, it was a different story in the North. Hindenburg used most of his reinforcements to form a new army, the Tenth (Herrmann von Eichhorn) on the northern flank of East Prussia. The Eighth (Otto von Below) was on its right (southern) flank, and, linked by patrols and light units, Mackensen's Ninth Army was on the extreme southern flank of the German line, facing Warsaw. His flank joined the Austrians, whose order of battle from north to south was the Second, First, Fourth, and Third Austrian armies. The Russian forces included the Tenth Army in the north, which held a line just across the East Prussian frontier; the Twelfth, just forming, northeast of Warsaw; the First and Second around Warsaw; and the Fifth, Fourth, Ninth, Third, Eighth, and Eleventh facing the Austrians.

Hindenburg's objective was destruction of the Tenth Russian Army and severance of one of the main Russian rail lines to Warsaw. Mackensen detached one corps to guard the flank of the Eighth Army farther north. He covered this movement with a masking attack at Bolimov on January 31. Bolimov, a drab Polish town on the railroad from Lodz to Warsaw, thus gained a kind of military immortality, for its name is forever associated with the first use of gas in war. The Germans fired some 18,000 tear gas shells against the Russians in their diversionary attack, but the intense cold and the primitive knowledge of chemical warfare limited effectiveness. A combination of reasons—lack of understanding of the weapon that had been used against them, and poor liaison—probably accounted for Russia's failure to inform her Western allies of the new weapon, so that the use of gas at Ypres on the Western Front some months later came as a partial surprise.

Mackensen's diversionary attack was successful in screening his troop movements, and Hindenburg was able to conceal the creation of his own Tenth Army from the enemy. Weather also contributed to surprise; the Eighth Army launched the offensive in a heavy snowstorm. The Winter Battle of Masuria (February 7 to 21) resulted in another great defeat for the Russians under conditions of incredible hardship for both sides. The German Tenth Army fell, like a scourge, against the northern flank of the Russian Tenth Army. In waist-deep snow drifts, and with frost-rimed horses straining at bogged-down guns, the Germans almost, but not quite, accomplished another double envelopment. The Russian XX Corps, surrounded in Augustow Forest, sacrificed itself for the three other corps of the Tenth Army. Total Russian losses were probably two hundred thousand—about half of them prisoners—and the Tenth Russian Army was out of action as an effective combat force for months to come. German combat losses were light, but the Russian winter—implacable enemy in other wars of Napoleon and of Hitler—exacted heavy toll.

It was another great tactical success, but strategic victory—the great double envelopment from north and south—had eluded the Central Powers. Like Antaeus, the Russians seemed to rise again stronger than ever each time they were hurled down.

Even Falkenhayn agreed in the spring of 1915 that it was now or never. The Austrian forces, dispirited, half-beaten, were near collapse; they had barely held, for a bloody month (March 18 to April 18), determined attempts by the Russian Third and Eighth armies to penetrate through the Carpathians to the Hungarian plain. Serbia, still fighting, flanked the communications to Turkey; Bulgaria and Rumania were uneasy neutrals. Peter was robbed to pay Paul.

The German Eleventh Army, newly formed on the Western Front, was shifted to the East, its detachment screened by a

German gas attack at Ypres on April 22. This army, with the Austrian Fourth, was placed under Mackensen and was positioned in great secrecy behind the Gorlice-Tarnow gap south of the Vistula. Elaborate supply and logistical preparations were made, and cover and deception were emphasized. German officers were disguised in Austrian uniforms, and in the extreme North, Hindenburg, relegated by Falkenhayn to a secondary role, launched a diversionary attack from East Prussia into Lithuania.

The Russians were ill prepared for the blow that was to come. About one third of the approximately six million Russian soldiers then in uniform had no rifles; many of them armed themselves in battle with the weapons of the fallen. Some were bootless. Ammunition shortages were so severe that expenditures were limited to about four rounds per gun a day. Small arms were of many makes from many nations. The Russian supply system was in chaos; corruption and laissez-faire tunneled, like termites, into the heart of the ponderous military machine. ". . . 1915 was for Russia the worst year of the war."[1]

The lightning struck on May 2, with almost one thousand guns—one to every fifty yards of front—battering the Russian lines from the Carpathians to the Vistula in the heaviest bombardment to date. The trench lines on the Eastern Front were in no way as formidable as in the West; trenches were shallow, dugouts relatively few; there was more room for maneuver. The Russian Third Army took the brunt of the surprise hammer blow; by May 4 it was virtually annihilated, and the breakthrough was accomplished. Mackensen advanced almost one hundred miles in two weeks; thousands of Russian prisoners were herded into the cages, dazed, uncomprehending. The entire Russian line was unhinged; the crests of the Carpathians, so hardly won, so briefly held, were abandoned.

From then until September, with but brief pauses, the Eastern Front was in almost continuous movement, as the Central Powers struck now here, now there, and the Russian withdrawal continued.

After the recapture of the fallen Austrian fortress of Przemysl on June 3, the German-Austrian forces were regrouped. In late June, with Lemberg captured, the Russian front looped westward in a great arc around Warsaw. To eliminate the remainder of the Polish salient, converging attacks from the south by Mackensen, from the north (East Prussia) by Max von Gallwitz's Twelfth Army (under Hindenburg) were launched. The Russian retreat—the plodding soldiers preceded by huge swarms of frightened refugees, a dust cloud marking their passing—was accelerated in August. Warsaw fell on August 4; the fortress of Brest-Litovsk was in German hands by the month's end. Hindenburg in the north captured Vilna, moved to the outskirts of Riga. By the end of September, when the Central Powers paused to consolidate for the winter, the Polish salient had been completely eliminated, Galicia regained, the Russian threat to the Hungarian plain apparently forever eliminated. The Eastern Front now ran for six hundred miles in an almost north-south line from the Dniester and the Rumanian frontier through the Pripet marshes to the Dvina.

It was a great defeat; hundreds of thousands of Russians were dead or wounded or caged in German or Austrian prison camps. The Grand Duke Nicholas, Russian supreme commander in the East, felt the ax, victim of the machinations of the court, the dry rot of the regime, and the disasters of the battlefield. The Czar, influenced by the Czarina, and through her by the mad monk, Rasputin, relieved his uncle of command, sent him to the Caucasus, and assumed personal command himself, with Mikhail Alexeiev as his chief of staff. Russia was still fighting, but the Czar had made his final major mistake.

For the Central Powers, the Eastern campaigns of 1915 fell short of finality and they smack too much of the "might-have-beens" of history. The friction between Falkenhayn and Hindenburg-Ludendorff-Conrad, born in part from opposing personal ambitions, handicapped the development of strategy, tended to produce temporizing decisions. The Germans had saved their Austrian allies; they had won great victories, but they were still locked in a death grip on two fronts.

The Western Front

Nineteen-fifteen was a year of deadlock and stalemate in the West. The Germans, on the strategic defensive, deployed nearly two million men in the trenches from Switzerland to the sea, confronting almost three million Allied soldiers. It was a year of build-up; the British Expeditionary Force expanded from ten to 37 divisions, the French to 107; the German order of battle in the West numbered almost one hundred divisions. But it was also a year of violent but futile assault upon a system of trenches, barbed wire, and field fortifications that constantly increased in strength.

There was no Allied supreme command and, in the full sense of the term, no concerted Allied grand strategy. The French, under Joffre, fresh from his victory of the Marne, were still imbued with the doctrine of the offensive; Joffre predicted in the spring he would be on the Rhine in the autumn.

There were many strategic schools of thought: some like Winston Churchill favored "eccentric strategy"—the use of British sea power to open new fronts on the flanks of Europe; some fertile minds were already seeking new weapons to overcome the bloody domination of the machine gun and barbed wire; many still felt breakthrough was possible on the Western Front with the help of massed artillery and massed men. The Allies defied the principle of military concentration and tried all the alternatives, thus dooming the plans in embryo. But the "Western Front" was generally dominant; Sir John French and later Sir Douglas Haig shared, with modifications, the views of Joffre and the French. So for month after month in 1915, and in the years to come, wave after wave of the young men of Europe died in futile horror, victims of a stubborn misconception.

Thus, the battles of 1915 in the West were more noted for slaughter than for accomplishment. The Allied attacks centered upon the so-called Noyon salient—the huge bulge in the German lines that protruded at its closest point to within about sixty miles of Paris. The winter and early spring battles were intended as rectifying or preliminary operations; the planned attacks later in the year culminating in the fall were envisaged as converging offensives on either flank of the Noyon bulge which, it was hoped, would eliminate it and force a major German retreat.

The French resumed their attacks in the Champagne area between Rheims and Massiges (west of Verdun) on February 15; the objective, the severance of a German railroad supply line five miles behind their lines. The insensate attacks continued until March 16; the French gained yards and lost thousands, though the Germans, too, died in droves. Neuve-Chapelle, on the Western flank of the Noyon bulge, was the next chronological blood bath (March 10-13). The British First Army, with the aid of extensive aerial photographs and large-scale trench maps, undertook a limited assault which was pretty effectively stopped in three hours after a thousand-yard advance. Cost: 3,266 British soldiers per hour.

Next was the Battle of the Woëvre (April 6-24), a futile attempt by the French First Army to reduce the St.-Mihiel salient, east of Verdun. "The results obtained were negligible and the great salient remained until the United States Army reduced it in September, 1918."[2]

On April 22, in the low-lying plains of Flanders, the Germans precipitated the Second Battle of Ypres when they used gas for the first time on the Western Front to cover the transfer of some of their troops from the West to the East. The Germans had made no plans for breakthrough; they initially mustered a local superiority against the French and British forces facing them, but they had few reserves. Gas was a tactical experiment. It was not wholly a surprise. Prisoners had talked, rumors had seeped out of Germany; a crude respirator (gas mask) had been captured. But the warnings to the higher command had gone unheeded, and most of the local commanders did not understand the significance of the intelligence they had garnered.

The Germans shelled the Ypres salient from early morning of the twenty-second, a lovely spring day. But it was not until about 5 P.M.—with the sun sinking in the west—that a yellowish-green mist, in appearance "such as is seen over water meadows on a frosty night,"[3] wafted slowly by the wind, seeped toward the trenches held by the 45th French Reserve Division (chiefly Algerian troops). It was chlorine, released from more than 5,700 metal cylinders. The French—choking, gasping, vomiting—ran in panic and opened a big gap on the flank of the 1st Canadian Division. Darkness, fear of the weapon they had used, and lack of planning to exploit the break, prevented effective follow-up by the Germans; next morning, the gap had been plugged by British reserves. Gas was used again on the twenty-fourth (and later in the battle). The Canadians, their mouths and noses wrapped in wet cloths, fought and died, many gasping for air. Second Ypres petered out by May 25 with gas an established weapon of war; the Allied salient reduced or abandoned, and with about 70,000 Allied casualties—the Germans half as many. Another opportunity at breakthrough had been lost.

The battles of Festubert, fought by the British (May 9-26), and Souchez, fought by the French (May 9-June 30) were local attacks on the western flank of the Noyon bulge between Neuve-Chapelle and Arras. Despite the costly lesson of almost a year of war, the British went over the top in ordered massed ranks and died the same way—mowed down by a scythe of lead. Gain: nothing. Loss: ten thousand men. The French at Souchez failed to capture Vimy Ridge, their objective, but punched a hole in the foremost German trench line, which was promptly filled by counterattack.

After a summer of recuperation, the Allies launched simultaneous assaults on September 25 from Artois and Champagne. In Artois, the British struck at Loos; the French resumed their assaults at Souchez toward Vimy Ridge, and in Champagne, west of Verdun, the French—with a three to one local superiority—attacked with more than thirty divisions on a front of about fifteen miles.

The Loos battle dragged on until October 14 but it was lost in the first few hours. The British First Army, Haig commanding, went over the top in an area pocked by mine pits and slag heaps and almost breached the German lines, but the reserves, with limited mobility, failed to follow through in time. Results: 60,000 British casualties; 20,000 Germans. It was the swan song for Sir John French; Lord Kitchener replaced him, in December, 1915, with Sir Douglas Haig.

The five-day battle of the French Tenth Army toward Vimy Ridge made limited gains, but when Joffre called it off the Germans still held most of the dominating high ground.

The Champagne attack, heralded by the largest artillery bombardment to date—a three-day bombardment by 2,500 guns—was broken early in October, although attacks continued until November 8. Gains in the first hours seemed good; several trench systems were penetrated but, as always, the penetrations could not be exploited, the battle could not be kept moving. Horsed cavalry, it was apparent, was not the answer. The French lost more than 150,000 men; the Germans over one hundred thousand.

That was all for 1915 in the West. It had been, for the Allies, a year of abortive hopes; the major gain (in yards) had been made by the Germans, with the aid of gas, in the reduction of the Ypres salient, but the front had not changed, anywhere, by more than three miles in either direction. Sir Douglas Haig, who took over top command of the three British armies in France at the year's end, thought the human attrition was justified; in the long run, Germany could not stand the strain. But to Lloyd George it was "bloody meaninglessness" and the Allies paid dearly. Their total casualties in the West were about 1,571,000 to 612,000 for the Germans.

The newfangled flying machine, something of a military novelty at war's beginning, became in 1915 an established part of the order of battle of all combatants. The airplane production of Germany, France, and Great Britain, John R. Cuneo estimates, increased from a total of 1,509 in 1914 (August to December) to 11,596 in 1915.[4] The nascent air power achieved its greatest strength on the Western Front, though it was used to a lesser extent—chiefly for reconnaissance and photography—in the East and in other theaters. The plane was employed for many functions over the deadlocked land front in the West, and it quickly developed in 1915, as the arms industries of all combatants were geared to war, to meet its new responsibilities. Air spotting for artillery fire—a function in which the plane was supplemented by the tethered balloon or blimp—was of major importance; reconnaissance reports aided the intelligence sections, and aerial photography helped the engineers map the battlefields. Air warfare inevitably followed, as each side tried to blind the enemy's "eyes."

The first British fighter reconnaissance squadron flew over the Western Front in July, 1915. During the early part of the year—and through midsummer—the German Air Force had been outclassed, numerically, in organization and technologically. But by October it had been reorganized and a monoplane, with a machine gun firing through the propeller, the product of a Dutch designer—the Fokker—was introduced and it soon established itself as queen of the air. Its development, and the corollary development of air tactics, sponsored individual air battles high above the trenches and excited the imagination of the world. Such names as Guynemer, Nungesser, Fonck, Richthofen, and later Bishop, Ball, McCudden, and others became world famous; they were the first "knights of the air."[5] But the totality—the extension of combat to behind-the-lines civilians which the plane was to bring to war—was an inevitable part of air power's growth. The Royal Flying Corps attempted to bomb German railway lines (in 1915 only a few attacks were successful). And German Zeppelins in raids on England as early as January, 1915, killed a number of British civilians. Paris was bombed in March, and the LZ-38 bombed London on May 1. Both combatants were learning that war in the twentieth century meant no holds barred.

THE DARDANELLES

Winston Churchill, First Lord of the Admiralty, had asked on Christmas Eve, 1914: "Are there not other alternatives than sending our armies to chew barbed wire in Flanders?"

Lord Fisher, the fiery First Sea Lord who had been recalled at seventy-four to replace Prince Louis of Battenberg, also favored "eccentric strategy," though his eyes were chiefly on the Baltic.

The concept of forcing the Dardanelles grew in many minds, but Churchill was its most persistent and prominent advocate. The promised rewards were immense: the outflanking of the Central Powers' interior position; the establishment of a secure supply line via the Black Sea to Russia; virtual elimination of Turkey from the war: the establishment of a Balkan front; help to Serbia; perhaps collapse of Austria-Hungary.

> The possession of the Dardanelles would have been the richest prize in the world for the Allies. . . . Admiral von Tirpitz (German naval minister) stated, in 1915, that "should the Dardanelles fall, then the World War has been decided against us."[6]

Such immense possibilities deserved careful planning and tremendous coordinated effort. But the political suspicions, which so often rend an Allied coalition, prevented close cooperation; Theodore Ropp has observed of Gallipoli that "as so often before and since, the Turks were to hold their capital because of jealousy among the Christians."[7] Nor was English planning adequate; the Dardanelles campaign, like Topsy, "jest growed"; vagueness and "lack of precision marked the War Council's deliberations."[8]

A combined amphibious operation was discussed—and though the concept was never wholly abandoned—it was shelved temporarily to permit the navy to try to force a passage.

The Dardanelles, a narrow, tortuous passage to the Sea of Marmara and Constantinople, was rather heavily defended in 1915, although many of its guns and fortifications were obsolescent. The narrow strait is flanked on the north by the Gallipoli peninsula—strategic keystone of the defense. A total of more than one hundred guns, up to fourteen inches in caliber, were sited from the entrance to the Sea of Mar-

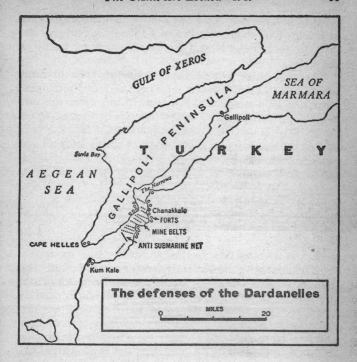

The defenses of the Dardanelles

mara, with the heaviest concentration at the Narrows, where the channel bottlenecks to a 1,600-yard width and curves sharply northward. Mine fields, covered by small guns and howitzers, and illuminated by searchlights, the whole augmented by torpedo tubes and an antisubmarine net, barred the sea passage. The Turks, aided by the prescient General Liman von Sanders, energetically strengthened this gantlet of fire, and prepared to contest the passage.

Vice Admiral Sackville Carden opened the ball on February 19 with eighteen major British ships, including the newly completed *Queen Elizabeth* (15-inch guns), and four

French battleships and auxiliaries. The one-day attack was resumed after a delay due to bad weather on February 25, and for a time it looked as if the navy alone might force the passage. The outer forts were silenced, and parties of blue-jackets landed at will and spiked the deserted Turkish guns near the strait's entrance.

But the attack bogged down; the British minesweepers, manned by fishermen, encountered heavy fire in the approach to the Narrows; the Turks took heart and drove off the roving landing parties. Carden, a sensitive man with little of the Nelsonian instinct, broke under the strain; he was invalided home on the verge of a nervous breakdown, and Vice Admiral John de Robeck took over.

On March 18, a grand assault was made and almost—but not quite—the thing was done. Before 2 P.M. the Turkish fire slackened and nearly died; the gunners were demoralized, some of the guns had been wrecked, communications destroyed, fire control impaired, ammunition nearly expended, less than thirty armor-piercing shells remained. But with startling reversal fate deserted the English; in quick succession the old French battleship *Bouvet* was sunk by a mine; *Inflexible* struck another mine, and the *Irresistible* still another. Later, the *Ocean* was fatally damaged by mine and shell fire. *Irresistible* and *Ocean* were abandoned in sinking condition in the face of the enemy, as the British withdrew. March 18, from grand beginning, drew on to puling end, and it was now the army's turn.

A British expeditionary force, hastily assembled, numbered initially about 78,000 men; its backbone, the Anzac (Australian-New Zealand) Corps. They were opposed by the newly constituted Turkish Fifth Army (astride the straits) of about 84,000 men, under von Sanders. General Sir Ian Hamilton, an elusive "British poet-general,"[9] commanded the Allied expeditionary force.

The landings on April 25 won some initial success. The key terrain feature at the narrow neck of the peninsula was almost seized by the Anzacs, but the tactical intuition and bold leadership of a Turkish division commander—Mustafa

Kemal, later to be known as Atatürk, the father of modern Turkey—drove them back. The initial beachheads were not vigorously exploited; leadership and generalship were found wanting, and Sir Ian Hamilton, though a charming gentleman and experienced soldier, failed to coordinate and direct the scattered landings with the crispness and decisiveness an amphibious operation requires.

It was to drag on for months, but the first few days determined the campaign's end. The beachheads, commanded by dominating enemy heights, were fire-swept; the outflanking operation intended to bypass the stalemate of the Western Front bogged down in trench warfare. Both sides attacked again and again, with minor gains but major losses. As the hot Mediterranean summer came on, the invaders began to go down with sickness: malaria and dysentery more than decimated the ranks! A Turkish destroyer torpedoed and sank the British battleship *Goliath* on the night of May 12-13, and a German U-boat torpedoed the *Triumph* and sank the *Majestic*. The Dardanelles were becoming an open, seeping wound.

But the British had the bull by the tail; they reinforced defeat and sent three more divisions to Hamilton. The Turks, too, built up; the Turkish Fifth Army numbered thirteen divisions by August when the British Army tried again. The August attacks, with a new landing at Suvla Bay, took place from August 6-10, but the objective—the dominating massif of Sari Bair, which the Anzacs had tried to reach in April—was still denied to the Allies. The rest was aftermath and predicament: how to face defeat and let go of the bull.

In September, one French and two British divisions were shifted to Salonika; in October, Hamilton was recalled and relieved by General Charles Monro. But it was not until November 23, with casualties from enemy fire and inexorable nature steadily mounting, that evacuation was decided upon after Lord Kitchener had visited Gallipoli. The evacuation began, in phases, in December, and despite tremendous anticipated losses it was successfully completed by January 8-9, 1916. The evacuation, ironically, was more brilliantly conducted by the British than any other phase of the campaign.

But no matter how the cake was sliced, it was a great defeat, "the worst British defeat between Saratoga and Singapore." Some 489,000 Allied soldiers were engaged; 252,000 were casualties. Of half a million Turks, 251,309 were killed, wounded, missing, died of disease, or were evacuated sick.[10] Gallipoli was also a maker and breaker of men and reputations: Kitchener's impeccable fame was tarnished, Lord Fisher resigned in May, Churchill was out soon afterward, Hamilton was through with soldiering forever, except for memoirs and memories. But Mustafa Kemal's star was on the rise; he was hailed as the "Savior of Gallipoli." In conception the Dardanelles expedition was sound; in execution, deplorable. It was, throughout, a history of too little and too late.

ITALY ENTERS THE WAR

Italy entered the struggle on May 23, but not on the side of her former allies, when she declared war against Austria. (More than a year later, August 27, 1916, she entered the list against Germany.) She brought into the conflict a favorable maritime geographic position at the narrow bottleneck of the Mediterranean, an unfavorable land battlefield, mass numbers, soldiers with peasant hardihood and Alpine skill, and General Count Luigi Cadorna, weather-beaten sixty-five-year-old chief of the Italian General Staff—a man with strategic grasp but deficient tactical understanding, good in organization, weak in the human touch, who was to drive Italian armies to their doom.

The Italian Army, deficient in supplies, machine guns, mortars, and modern equipment, mobilized at the start about 870,000 officers and men. Her navy, though small, was favored by geography; Italy's entrance into the war put the cork in the bottle of the Adriatic Sea and finally doomed the Austro-Hungarian Navy to the slow death of blockade.

But for Italy the only land battlefield available—her rugged northern frontier, more than four hundred miles long from Switzerland to the Adriatic—was almost impossibly difficult. The terrain alone was majestically formidable; to the difficulties of nature, the Austrians had added the handiwork of man. Even prior to hostilities the Austrians, with a justifiable mistrust of their pseudo-ally, had seamed the frontier with field fortifications.

Geography, always the arbiter of strategy, also favored Austria. The Austrian positions in the great enclave of the Trentino, just east of Switzerland, extended like a dagger into northern Italy. The Austrians occupied the heights; below them stretched the rich valley of the Po and the vital Italian lateral rail lines from Brescia to Verona, Treviso, and Udine. To the east of the Trentino, the high peaks of the Alps and a tangled maze of mountains forbade assault. There was left the Isonzo front with Trieste and an approach to the Ljubljana Gap leading to the Austro-Hungarian plain as the objectives. It was here that Italy and Cadorna chose to stake their fate in bloody battering battle after battle, conscious always that behind their backs in the Trentino the poised Austrians might at any time erupt to cut their main lines of supply. Italy fought the war uphill.

The Italians mustered thirty-six divisions on mobilization day; the Austrians along the frontier were outnumbered heavily. But the Gorlice-Tarnow breakthrough in the East had already won smashing successes; before June 23, when the Italians jumped off in the First Battle of the Isonzo, Vienna had twenty divisions on or near the Italian Front, under the Archduke Eugen.

Cadorna's chosen battlefield, where he was to launch in 1915 the first four of a total of twelve attacks, has been variously described as a "howling wilderness of stones . . ." and "the strongest fortified area ever attacked by man." The Isonzo flows north and south; the key sectors were the Carso plateau near the river's debouchment into the Adriatic; Gorizia, a town dominated by high peaks; and the Upper Isonzo, a lowering, deep-trenched gorge beneath peaks as high as 7,300 feet. Italians, attacking the heights across the deep river trench, found, to paraphrase the words of Dr.

Douglas W. Johnson (in *Topography and Strategy in War*) that they could not cross the river until they had captured the mountains and they could not reach the mountains until they had crossed the river.

This dilemma capsules all of the battles of the Isonzo. The first four—really one intermittent battle—occurred from June 23–July 7, July 18–September 30, October 18–November 4, and November 10-12.

Meanwhile, in the Trentino and the Alps, the Italians undertook a holding offensive and minor tactical assaults to improve their front-line positions.

The gains everywhere were minuscule, the losses huge; more than a quarter of a million Italian casualties on all fronts during 1915, 161,000 of them in the four Isonzo battles. The Austrians suffered, too; more than 160,000 men killed, wounded, missing, or captured. But Cadorna's assaults, ever bigger and bigger as more men, divisions, and guns paid homage to death, did not even save Serbia.

THE DEATH OF SERBIA—SALONIKA

The famous route of the Orient Express—which the Kaiser had hoped someday would become the chief link in the vaunted "Berlin to Baghdad Railway"—passed through Serbia. In fact the little country, armed and fighting, exercised a veto power over the supply routes of the Central Powers and over German strategy in the Balkans. Rumania was restive; Turkey had to be helped; Serbia stood in the way.

Falkenhayn became convinced that Serbia must be liquidated and Bulgaria recruited. The Gorlice-Tarnow breakthrough, the futile assaults of the Italians, and the repulse of the British at the Dardanelles persuaded Bulgaria; she "signed up" secretly on September 6, mobilized on September 21, attacked Serbia's eastern flank on October 11, and was to muster before the war was over about 1,200,000 men.

The death blow to Serbia was planned by the same German staff officer, Colonel Hentsch, whose actions at the Battle of the Marne had provided the stuff of controversy. Von

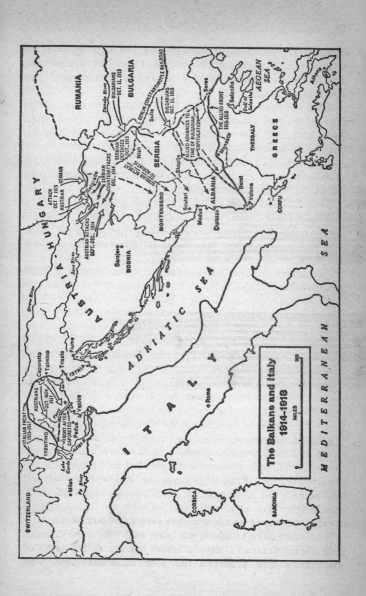

The Balkans and Italy
1914-1918

Mackensen, promoted to field marshal, directed three of the four armies—the Austrian Third, the German Eleventh (shifted from the Russian front), and the Bulgarian First. The Germans and Austrians attacked from the north, the Bulgarians from the east. An additional Bulgarian Army— the Second, operating directly under Sofia's control—drove into Serbia in the southeast to cut the railroad to Salonika.

The Austrians and Germans attacked on October 6; the Bulgarians, against the Serbian flank and rear on the eleventh. . The Serbs were outnumbered at least three to two, and completely outclassed in artillery and in other weapons. Vulnerable Belgrade fell on October 9, never to be regained by a nation named Serbia. By October 18, with the Bulgarian Army crossing their eastern frontier and severing the Serbs' communications to Greece, Serbia was in the last throes. For a time hope gleamed, but briefly.

The Allies had anticipated the blow. On October 3, the vanguard of a three-division Allied expeditionary force, the bulk of the troops transferred from Gallipoli, landed at the Greek port of Salonika, under the nominal over-all command of the French General Maurice Sarrail. Greece was theoretically neutral, although the pro-Allied Premier Eleutherios Venizelos, encouraged the landing. Venizelos, however, fell from power soon after Salonika was occupied and the expedition was beset from the beginning with political differences, the lack of a clear-cut purpose, and command problems. The Allies were again too little and too late.

The severance of the rail route to Salonika by the Bulgarian Second Army (by the capture of Veles and Kumanovo on October 23) prevented the juncture of Sarrail's force and the hard-pressed Serbs. The Allies retreated to Salonika, where they stubbornly wired themselves into a defensive sanctuary dubbed the "Bird Cage," prepared against attack by either the Bulgars or the uncertain Greeks.

The remnants of the Serbian Army, in one of the epic fighting retreats of history, retired in a bloody odyssey across the snow-covered, bitter mountains to the Albanian coast, taking 23,000 Austrian prisoners with them. They debouched from the mountain passes to the thin edge of the Adriatic, "dirty skeletons in rags," voraciously munching raw cabbage and candles and anything edible.[11] The survivors, perhaps 140,000 men, were transported chiefly by the French and Italians from the ports of Valona and Durazzo to Greek Corfu for recuperation and reorganization. They left behind them one hundred thousand dead or wounded and 160,000 prisoners. Many who lived to fight again were emaciated, with pipestem legs and harrowed features; the nurses at Corfu could easily lift grown men in their arms.

The Austrians, attacking through Montenegro, followed hard on the heels of the vanquished Serbs. Montenegro was quickly overrun and surrendered on January 17, 1916. Most of Albania was also occupied, except for the southern portion, held by Italian troops, who had come not only to rescue the Serbian remnants but to establish a political beachhead on the eastern shore of the Adriatic Sea.

The Outer Theaters

Great oaks from little acorns grow. The British involvement in Mesopotamia, like their involvement at Gallipoli and Salonika, increased imperceptibly as minor triumphs fed political ambitions, and unsated appetite for glory led to disaster.

The Indian Army, conducting its own campaign under loose directions from London and a tighter rein from New Delhi, opposed in Mesopotamia a combination of Turks and Arabs and Kurds. The original British investment was small and the motives sound—to guard the oil wells at the head of the Persian Gulf. But from Basra, occupied toward the end of 1914, the British pushed northward up the Tigris and Euphrates, lured by the glittering mirage of the city of the Arabian Nights—Baghdad. An army corps under General John Nixon, with General Charles Townshend in command of the Sixth Indian Division, reinforced, started the move inland in June, after repulsing in April an attack at Nasiriya by some twenty thousand Turks. At Kut al Imara on Sep-

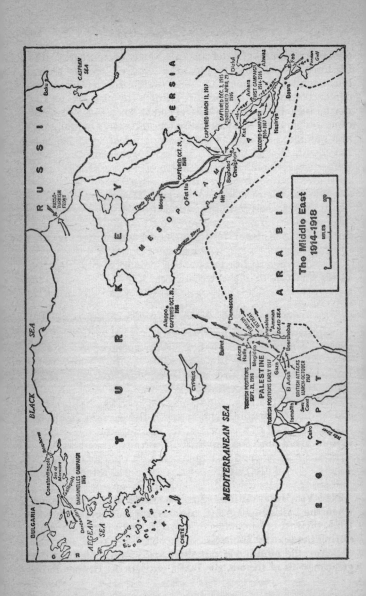

The Middle East
1914-1918

tember 28 Townshend defeated a strongly entrenched Turkish force. The British should have left well enough alone, but Baghdad beckoned and the overconfident Nixon ordered Townshend, against his wishes, to push on to the north. In a four-day battle (November 22-26), Townshend came a cropper despite a limited tactical success at Ctesiphon, and was forced to retreat with his exhausted troops to Kut. Here, with but few supplies, Townshend and his 8,800 men were to meet their Calvary. They were beleaguered and encircled and besieged by a Turkish-Arab army, under the top strategic direction of Field Marshal Kolmar von der Goltz, supreme commander for the Central Powers in Mesopotamia. The alarm went out, and as 1915 ended, a relief force mobilized farther south, prepared to fight its way to Townshend.

In the meantime, the Turkish commander in Syria, Djemal Pasha, had had the audacity in February, 1915, to threaten the Suez Canal. In a remarkable advance across 120 miles of the waterless Sinai desert, some 15,000 to 20,000 Turks—hauling pontoons and guns with them—reached the east (Sinai) bank of the canal. Some even crossed into Egypt proper. The attack was repulsed, but the scare had left its mark; for the rest of 1915, thousands of Allied troops poured into Egypt.

In German East Africa, where Lettow-Vorbeck was still playing fox to the British hounds, the cruiser *Königsberg*, damaged and holed up in the Rufiji River, was finally destroyed in July, with the aid of air spotting and two British monitors sent out from England.

THE WAR AT SEA

New Year's Day, 1915, forecast the shape of things to come when the battleship *Formidable* was lost in home waters to U-24, the first of a number of British men-of-war to be sunk during the year by U-boats.

Before the month was out there was another clash of the great mastiffs of the sea, the battle cruisers. At Dogger Bank in the North Sea a German squadron was intercepted by Beatty on January 24. The Germans, under Hipper, were overmatched in weight of broadside about two to one. Battle cruisers *Seydlitz, Moltke* and *Derfflinger,* and *Blücher,* an armored cruiser with 8.2-inch guns, screened by four light cruisers and nineteen destroyers, met in a running fight Beatty's battle cruisers, *Lion, Tiger, Princess Royal, New Zealand,* and *Indomitable,* with seven light cruisers and thirty-five destroyers. Hipper turned tail for Heligoland as soon as he was sighted, and for four hours it was a stern chase. *Blücher,* the weakest ship in the squadron, was the last ship in Hipper's column, and she was pounded heavily as the British van slowly overtook the retiring Germans. *Lion,* Beatty's flag in the van of the British line, was the target for many German guns, and took many hits. At 9:43 A.M., *Seydlitz,* steaming hard, took a 13.5-inch hit from *Lion* in the after barbette. The shell ignited powder charges in the ammunition hoists, snuffed out the lives of 159 men, put the two after turrets out of action, and sent a funereal pall of smoke and flame hundreds of feet into the air. *Seydlitz* was saved "by the bravery of a chief petty officer."

> The wheels actuating the flooding valves [to the magazines] were red hot, but he gripped them and turned them, though they burnt the very flesh off his hands and he suffered cruelly.[12]

Blücher took what proved to be a mortal hit shortly after 10:30, which put her two forward 8.2-inch turrets out of action, damaged boilers and steering gear, and turned the ship into an inferno. She dropped rapidly behind, sheered out of line, and was left alone to her fate.

Lion, in the van, was badly pounded; one shell set her forward magazine afire; she was saved by flooding. As she slowed and dropped out of the fight, Beatty's second-in-command misunderstood a message from his chief, and instead of pursuing Hipper concentrated on damaged *Blücher.* The German cruiser—like most other German ships in the war—was tough; she took seven torpedoes and perhaps one hundred shell hits before she sank at 12:13 P.M., firing to the last. It was a British victory but also an opportunity lost. *Lion* got back to port for patching, and her personnel losses—despite bad damages—were remarkably light. The Germans lost 951 dead, all on the *Blücher* and *Seydlitz.*

February, 1915, marked the start of intensified submarine warfare. There were then only twenty-seven U-boats ready for action but they quickly made history. On May 7, in the Irish Sea, U-20 (*Schweiger*) sank the fast Cunarder *Lusitania,* unarmed, but with ammunition and more than a thousand passengers (440 women and children) aboard. One hundred and fifteen American citizens died. The *Lusitania's* sinking made a tremendous psychological impression upon the world; in the United States "Remember the *Lusitania*" became, in time, a rallying cry for war. Other incidents and a bitter exchange of notes between Washington and Berlin followed and turned American enmity toward Germany. Grudgingly, the Germans finally promised limitations on their submarine campaign. Nevertheless, the toll of Allied shipping sunk by the Central Powers increased steadily in 1915 from 59,900 tons in February to a peak of 185,800 tons in August (including shipping sunk by surface raiders). But not without counterloss. Several U-boats were sunk, among them U-29, skippered by Otto Weddigen, who had won immortal fame in a few short months of war by sinking (in U-9) *Aboukir, Cressy,* and *Hogue* and later the cruiser *Hawke.* The U-29 was rammed and sunk on March 25 by the British *Dreadnought.* And two could play at the same game. British submarines which had been operating amidst mines and shoals in the dangerous Baltic since the late months of 1914 found good pickings.

The entry of Italy into the war led in the Adriatic to a series of raids and counterraids by both sides. The Austrians, operating from excellent heavily fortified deep water bases at Sibernik, Pola, and Cattaro, shelled the Italian coast and the Italians retaliated. The Italian Navy, though reinforced by British and French ships, suffered somewhat heavier losses in the attrition attacks of 1915. The cruisers *Amalfi* and *Garibaldi* were lost to U-boats (July 7, July 18), and submarines and other ships of both sides were damaged or sunk, including the French cruiser *Leon Gambetta* (April 26-27). The Adriatic was a sea which neither side completely commanded in 1915; nevertheless, the Austrian surface fleet was restricted to its waters and played no part in the Mediterranean and the Allies were able to evacuate Serbian troops from Adriatic ports. In the fall, the British, with Allied aid, commenced to lay a net and mine barrage across the Otranto Strait in an attempt—ineffective at first—to bottle up the U-boats.

Nineteen-fifteen was a year of flowing blood and small comfort for the Allies. In Britain, the star of Lloyd George was rising; Herbert Asquith formed a coalition cabinet; Churchill went off to fight in the trenches. Russia suffered her greatest casualties of the war—perhaps two million killed and wounded; another 1,300,000 in German prison pens.[13] Serbia was overrun; the Salonika expedition locked up in what Berlin scornfully called "their largest internment camp."

The Central Powers had established a secure fortress, a central position with continuous communications and lines of supply from one partner to another. Gallipoli had been a disaster. The Western Front, after more than two million casualties, was still in stalemate. Townshend was besieged in a blowzy Arab town named Kut that few Englishmen had ever heard of. And the submarine was ravaging the shipping lanes. It had been a year of missed opportunities and increasing hatred; slowly the comprehension of the meaning of Total War was dawning on the world.

IV

STRUGGLE OF ATTRITION—1916

In 1916, God—it became clear—was on the side of the Big Factories as well as the Big Battalions. Industrial mobilization, a new term in the military dictionary, harnessed the factories of the belligerents to the maw of war, supervised the farms, taxed incomes, rationed food. Prodigious quantities of ammunition and war equipment poured from the machines; yet ever more was always needed. Britain, mistress of the oceans, Britain, which "had fed her sea for a thousand years," commenced, too, to feed the land; in January, she adopted conscription for the first time in her history and committed herself to a mass army. It was a decision which was to have profound effect upon the war and also upon the future of England; it was to mean, indeed, the beginning of the end of Britain's long predominance as a world power. The war entered an attrition phase of vast killings on the Western Front. In the East a great Russian offensive spelled the beginning of the end for two great monarchies which had outlived their time. Avaricious Rumania entered the war, strutted for her brief moment in the sun, and succumbed. Jutland, the war's greatest naval battle, was fought to indeterminate conclusion. The pressure of the blockade drew its coils tighter around the Central Powers. Leaders fell from power, and in many a home from Russian steppe to Cotswold cottage, men became memories; hatred thickened.

The Western Front

The pendulum of war swung back from East to West in 1916, as two of the greatest battles of history—Verdun and the Somme—enlisted the strength of empires.

There had been little strategic coordination among the Allies in the first years of the war; there was a history of cross-purposes and suspicions, political ambitions and doubts. The first attempt to achieve better coalition planning occurred in December, 1915, under the cloak of the immense prestige of Joffre. French, British, Belgian, Italian, Russian, and even Japanese representatives discussed the future and agreed, in principle, upon simultaneous offensives during 1916 on the Italian front and in West and East.

But this plan, like so many others in the capacious files of war, was stillborn when the Germans beat the Allies to the punch.

Falkenhayn, whose eyes had always been turned toward the West, mobilized his major effort. Whether or not he believed in breakthrough—he wrote that it was unnecessary —he girded for it. He was prepared to bleed France white, to pick a point of attack "for the retention of which [in his own words] the French command would be compelled to throw in every man they have." Verdun was his deliberate selection. It was a keystone of the French front and of immense moral and psychological significance to France.

Falkenhayn based his offensive on new tactics. He assembled a tremendous mass of artillery, including the heaviest guns available—12-inch naval rifles and 420-mm. siege mortars. Bombardments unprecedented in the history of war were to pulverize the French defenses and chew up French counterattacks. In effect, the artillery would take the ground; the infantry, attacking on a narrow front, would simply consolidate and occupy it. As a German staff study stated, "The decision to attack and rapidly seize Verdun is based on the proven effects of heavy and heaviest artillery."[1]

These tactics stemmed in part from the experiences of the early years of the war when fortresses at Liége, Namur, and Maubeuge, and later Russian forts, had succumbed rather quickly to German *schwere* (heavy) artillery. Verdun, as a king post in the French fortified zone, had been, in 1914, a maze of steel and concrete forts with heavy guns and machine-gun posts—all sited in mutually supporting concentric circles radiating outward from the old town. Curiously enough, the same "lessons" that had impressed the Germans impressed the French; Verdun had been a quiet sector from late 1914 to 1916, and at Joffre's direction the formidable forts had been largely stripped and abandoned; some of them had been prepared for demolition and troop strength greatly reduced. The French defensive strength at the beginning of 1916 was based largely upon the difficult terrain—"like a great natural fortress"—astride the Meuse River and a spotty, but in places very strong, system of field fortifications—dugouts, log and earth bunkers, machine-gun emplacements, and trenches protected by thirty to forty feet of tangled barbed wire paralleled by another barrier or *abattis* of wooden and iron stakes and a maze of wire six feet high and twenty feet wide.

The French intelligence had secured ample warning of the impending attack; indeed, the German mobilization was so massive that it could not be concealed. But the French were engrossed in their own plans for an offensive and Joffre believed the Germans planned an attack elsewhere. Weather saved them. The German attack, originally scheduled for February 12, had to be postponed because of drab, rainy weather which blotted out the field of fire of the German artillery O.P.'s (observation points). By February 21 the French had increased their strength in the vulnerable north-east sector where the heaviest German blow fell from one brigade to two divisions. Even so, they were outnumbered about three or four to one in early morning on February 21 when the greatest bombardment in the history of warfare put to test the theories of Falkenhayn and the Greater German General Staff.

Before the German infantry went "over the top" (of their trenches), the staff briefing officers of the attacking units had been confident.

"There won't be anything left living out there. . . ."

But they were wrong. In the dusk of that February afternoon the assault units on a thirty-five-mile front met spotty yet unexpectedly strong resistance. The French *mitrailleuses* still chattered, the *poilus* still stood and died. The advance was slow, inching. The Germans called upon a new weapon, the flame-thrower, to rout the French from their bunkers. The *Sturmbataillon Rohr*, "elite of the elite, the tough, battle-tried trench busters . . . armored like knights of old and carrying small mortars and flame-throwers,"[2] tried their hand.

They, too, proved mortal.

For almost eight days the Germans edged inward around the apex of the great salient that enclosed Verdun. The nearest front line was eight miles from the city when the assault started. By the end of February, the German attack at the closest point had almost halved this distance. Fort Douaumont, a major link in the chain of forts around Verdun, was seized by the Germans on the twenty-fifth, unoccupied. Fort or no fort, it was a key position and many men were yet to die attacking or defending it. On the eastern flank the French withdrew to the heights of the Meuse, but Joffre, under political fire from the Briand government, forbade any further retreat: "Any commander who under the circumstances gives orders to retreat will be brought before a court-martial."

The French held, but it had been a near thing.

At midnight, February 25-26, just before the first German attack had spent itself, a general named Henri P. Pétain, who was to win fame and adulation at Verdun in World War I and hatred and ignominy at Vichy in World War II, took command of the whole Verdun salient.

His energy, tactical skill, and determination infused the defense with new life. The French were heavily reinforced with guns and men; searching counterbattery fire harried the German gunners. The abandoned forts, most of them little damaged by the German artillery, were reoccupied. Supply was reorganized.

Supply was the key to the French position. Verdun was

in a cul-de-sac, the salient split by the Meuse River. One standard-gauge and one narrow-gauge railway, frequently cut by German artillery fire, and one key road—*La Voie Sacrée* (The Sacred Way)—supplied 437,000 troops and 136,000 horses and mules. *La Voie Sacrée* was carefully organized and maintained. Like the "Red Ball Express" of World War II, truck convoys—at peak capacity one truck every fourteen seconds—rolled day and night along The Sacred Way.[3] The internal combustion engine was changing the art of war, and for the French, Verdun was a triumph of supply as well as of will.

After a lull, the Germans tried again on March 6, this time with the main effort to the west of the Meuse. Throughout March and April in snow and mist and spring rain, the Crown Prince of Prussia, commanding the German Fifth Army, drove his men toward Verdun. Hill Mort Homme and Hill 304, Fort Douaumont and Fort Vaux, the latter one of the keys to the Heights of the Meuse on the east bank, were household words in 1916. They were attacked, counterattacked, smashed, chivvied, assaulted, blasted, taken, and retaken.

The terrible artillery fire dazed and stunned and destroyed, but it did not conquer.

> The landscape assumed a lunar aspect, an unending succession of shell craters, some immense. The woodlands were reduced to a debris of tangled, shattered boughs amid stumps. Here and there rotting bodies of men and horses protruded from the churned and tortured soil. As the weather grew warmer the stench of carrion became more disgusting. Troops left long in this inferno appeared to age. Their eyes sank in their heads; their features became drawn.[4]

Until July Falkenhayn and the Crown Prince kept trying; on June 21 they tried a new form of poison gas—diphosgene. But Pétain, now in command of the Army Group of the Center, with General Robert Georges Nivelle under him in command of the salient, had sounded the keynote: *"On les aura!"*

The failure of February capsuled for the Germans the

failures of the months to come.

It was the French turn from August almost to year's end. In October and December, under fiery General Charles Mangin, carefully prepared attacks regained Forts Vaux and Douaumont and pushed back the high tide—frothed with blood—of the German assault upon Verdun.

Verdun, an epic of resistance, was one of the most sanguinary battles of the war. In one sense Falkenhayn had been right: it had claimed many of France's bravest and best— 460,000 French casualties. But the Germans had paid with almost 300,000 men.

There are some who think Verdun was saved by the Battle of the Somme. There is, indeed, a coincidence in dates of crisis. The Somme offensive started on July 1 (postponed, because of weather, from June 29), shortly after the Germans made their final major effort to dominate the Heights of the Meuse. And the Somme offensive had gradually been transformed in the first half of 1916 from an attempt at breakthrough and victory to a counteroffensive intended in part to relieve the pressure on Verdun. Originally the French were to have made the main effort; Verdun changed that— the British shouldered the burden. Nevertheless, in retrospect Verdun won its own victory; the Somme was a supplement.

The British attacked with twelve divisions, plus seven in reserve, on a front of fifteen miles. The Fourth Army was their spearhead, supported by the French Sixth Army, with five divisions on a six-mile front, on its flank. The Allies were aided by air superiority. At the start of the Battle of Verdun, the Fokker was supreme, but by July, 1916, the French Nieuport and the British De Havilland Scout had redressed the balance and German aerial reconnaissance was blinded. The battle also marked the appearance of antiaircraft guns in some numbers. The British and French were opposed by elements of the German Second Army, and, more important, by formidable defenses. The Somme sector had been fortified and developed for two years. As Sir Douglas

Haig pointed out in his dispatches, the Germans "had spared no pains to render these defenses impregnable." Fortified villages, deep dugouts in the chalk, interlocking barriers of iron stakes and barbed wire, deep cellars, underground shelters and passageways had made the Somme sector one of the "strongest and most perfectly defended in the world."

Joffre had selected it as an area of attack, as Falkenhayn had selected Verdun. It was his mistake.

The assault opened, as usual, with the heaviest artillery concentration to date; each succeeding battle on the Western Front exceeded in superlatives the dread statistics of the past. But the Germans simply took shelter in their secure dugouts, watched with periscopes as the British went "over the top" and, as soon as the barrage lifted, moved their machine guns into position.

The British attacked in waves, "the men in each, almost shoulder to shoulder in a symmetrical, well-dressed alignment," moving "at a slow walk with their rifles held aslant. . . ."[5]

The result was slaughter—more than 60,000 British casualties killed, wounded, prisoners, and missing in one day, the worst day of any war for the British Army.

The French did somewhat better; however, nowhere was there even a semblance of a breakthrough. But Haig bulled ahead. In a succession of small attacks by day and by night for five months, the Allies drove a salient or bulge about five miles in depth into the German lines astride the Somme from the vicinity of Péronne to Beaumont. Trench lines and barbed wire were obliterated; shell holes pocked the face of the land; the stench of death fouled the air.

On September 15, the British, like the Germans before them, hatched a new weapon. This time it was the tank. A strange, ungainly armored vehicle, crawling on caterpillar treads, it had been developed partially because of the enthusiasm and interest of the former First Lord of the Admiralty, Winston Churchill. The tank stemmed from the operations of a naval armored car detachment in France in the early days of the war.

It mated the American caterpillar tracks with armor and guns, and was intended as a means of meeting the machine gun and of crushing barbed wire. The term "tank" was purely fortuitous—a name given in place of "land ship" or "land cruiser" to preserve secrecy. Lieutenant Colonel E. D. Swinton, who with Churchill and others must be given credit for the development of the tank, and his colleague, Lieutenant Colonel W. Dally Jones, considered "such terms as 'container,' 'reservoir,' 'cistern,' " but decided on the word "tank" as being "short and ambiguous."[6] It stuck through many wars and battles.

Thirty-six tanks, "male" (mounting six-pounder guns) and "female" (mounting machine guns), attacked in the van of twelve divisions, including the Canadian Corps in its first big battle. A painful bloody mile and a half was gained. The rumbling steel monsters made a mighty impression on both friend and foe, but there were too few of them, and they were too unreliable mechanically to score decisively.

Thus, the battlefield debut of the tank—a great new weapon—was wasted, as gas had been. It was committed too soon, partly in answer to pressure from Haig. It rumbled into battle before it was fully developed and before the men who handled it were fully trained. And it was directed by generals who did not understand its use.

Weather—torrential rains in October and early November —ended the battle of the Somme. The ground, scarred and tortured by continuous shell fire, became a morass; to live was an ordeal, to fight impossible.

Verdun and the Somme, with their infernos of fire, bled both sides white. The British and French lost about 1,200,000 men (total casualties of all types) in 1916 on the Western Front; the Germans, 800,000. From the Allied point of view the bloodletting was not wholly negative. Ludendorff later wrote (partly in self-exculpation) that 1916 "completely exhausted" the German Army on the Western Front. Falkenhayn, apostle of attrition, was a victim of his own strategy. He was relieved as chief of staff in late August, and Hindenburg and Ludendorff, fresh from triumphs in the East, took the helm.

It was the end, too, for Joffre's days of glory. His intractable stubbornness and free-ranging interference in political matters—as well as Verdun and the Somme—contributed to his downfall. Premier Briand promoted him to Marshal of France and sent him into retirement, where time could never tarnish, nor history dull, his accomplishments. General Nivelle, young, volatile, promising great things, was chosen to succeed him.

THE EASTERN FRONT

By March, 1916, the Russians had filled up their ranks, riddled by 1915's defeats, and had produced and imported enough infantry weapons to arm their new contingents.

Again, as in 1914, the Czar's forces started the year's campaigns cast in a sacrificial role. Verdun was the cause; the French appeal to the Czar for a diversion led to a hasty, ill-prepared assault by the Russian Second Army against strong German positions near Lake Naroch (March 18-26). Mud and cold and blunder, and German artillery and machine-gun fire stopped the "steam roller" once again after indecisive gains, and the Czar had close to 100,000 more casualties, with nothing to show for it.

There followed a lull in the East with preparations for a great coordinated offensive. But it was not to be. Once again stress in the West—this time an Austrian offensive in Italy in May—led to a premature decision to attack. It was to be the last great action of the war for Russia, and unlike the others, it was to lead to at least a Pyrrhic victory. Alexey Brusilov, a fiery, courageous, and able cavalryman—perhaps the best of the Russian generals—led it, and the offensive has come to be named for him. Brusilov in 1916 commanded the Southwestern Army Group, which he volunteered to commit to the offensive against the Austrians in June in answer to the Italians' appeal for aid. He commanded the Seventh, Eighth, Ninth, and Eleventh armies, with a total of more than fifty divisions. He faced on a two-hundred-mile front four largely Austrian armies (strengthened by a few German divisions), numbering forty-six divisions.

Brusilov launched his main efforts, cloaked by surprise, north of Dubno and near the Dniester River, close to the Rumanian frontier. The offensive jumped off on June 4; by the following day the Austrians, with no stomach for the fight, were in trouble. The Austrian Fourth Army in the north and the Seventh in the south collapsed physically and morally; the dissident minorities in the Austro-Hungarian empire (now the majority in the ranks of the army) simply took off for the rear or fraternized with their Slavic cousins in the Russian units.

Brusilov's first drive spent itself by mid-June. But, despite customary supply shortages and transport difficulties and the failure of Russia's other army groups to launch a promised supporting offensive, Brusilov moved again to the attack. By late June, the dimensions of his victory had grown, for the Austrians, to a near catastrophe. The Austrian Fourth and Seventh armies on the flanks had been completely routed; the Russians had almost reached the passes through the Carpathians and the tottering empire of Austria-Hungary had sustained hundreds of thousands of casualties.

But the extent of the Brusilov triumph triggered a frantic reaction. Hindenburg and Ludendorff scooped up all the divisions they could spare along the Eastern Front to plug the breakthroughs. German divisions were transferred from the West (weakening the attack on Verdun), and Austrian reinforcements came from the Italian front (ending the Austrian drive into Italy). The defense stiffened. Brusilov bulled ahead in August and September, but at terrible cost—the Russians, attacking in mass formations, were mowed down like rows of ripe corn. Again Russian supply services failed to support their armies; men advanced, barehanded, into battle to die in mangled heaps, tearing with bleeding hands at the barbed wire.

It was all over by the time the leaves turned crimson and gold as both sides slumped in exhaustion.

The Brusilov offensive was the greatest Russian victory

of the war. It inflicted about 600,000 casualties, including about 400,000 prisoners, against the hapless Austrians and brought some strategic relief both to the Italian and the Western fronts. But at huge cost: almost one million dead, wounded, prisoners, missing, and deserted; the morale of an army shattered; and the Russian *muzhiks* ripe for revolution. Brusilov's victory drove the Austro-Hungarian empire to the verge of destruction, but it carried within it the seeds of Russia's fall.

Prophetically, Francis Joseph I, Emperor of Austria and King of Hungary, died in November at eighty-six, depressed by defeat. He was the last of the *ancien régime;* his sixty-seven-year reign, ending in the world's largest war, had seen the great and near-great of two centuries pass across the stage of history. Mercifully, he was spared the culminating tragedy—the breakup of the empire he had ruled.

RUMANIA

The desire of men for glory and of governments for gain was the familiar reason for Rumania's belated entry into the war. Like Italy, she reneged in 1914 on her treaty with Austria, interpreting it to suit the convenience of Bucharest. For two years she vacillated between caution and greed, until finally on August 27, 1916, stimulated by Brusilov's successes and attracted by Allied promises of territorial gains, she declared war upon Austria. (Germany and Bulgaria quickly added Rumania to their formal list of enemies.)

Rumania's grain and oil were glittering economic prizes, but her L-shaped geographic position—virtually surrounded by enemies, with her capital only thirty miles from a dangerous frontier—was vulnerable. Her half-million-man army —twenty-three divisions with more mobilizing—was a dubious asset, led by generals who knew nothing of war, some of them corseted and rouged martinets.

Rumania started with attacks to the west and north: her objective, beyond the mountain passes of the Carpathians and the Transylvanian Alps, the glittering prize of Transylvania in the Hungarian plain.

Three of Rumania's four armies were committed to a drive through widely separated passes and over bad roads on a two-hundred-mile front. By mid-September stiffening Austrian resistance, Rumanian caution and ineptitude, and supply difficulties bogged down the offensive after a fifty-mile advance.

And, far to the rear and south, peril threatened. Rumania's defection had been anticipated by the Central Powers. Von Mackensen, German conqueror of Serbia, had raised a German, Bulgarian, and Turkish Danube army, which invaded Dobruja province on September 1. And in Transylvania, two Austro-German armies—the First and the Ninth—were to be ready by September 30. The Ninth was commanded by Falkenhayn, deposed chief of the German General Staff.

Von Mackensen pushed a two-prong drive northward— one along the Danube, another near the Black Sea. By mid-September, after capturing fortified Tutrakan and Silistra, he was approaching the Constanta-Cernavoda-Bucharest railway, Rumania's only rail link to the Black Sea. Here, faced by a strong Russian-Rumanian force in good defensive positions, Mackensen was halted.

But his advance, coupled with an intermittent air bombardment of Bucharest to which the Rumanians could offer no defense (they had no airplanes and virtually no anti-aircraft guns), brought fear to the capital. The Transylvanian drive was weakened to reinforce the Dobruja and the Bulgarian front. Yet the Rumanian planners tried to have their cake and eat it, too. They decided to continue the Transylvanian drive, and simultaneously to strike south and east across the Danube against Mackensen's rear. There were sufficient troops for one but not for both. Both, therefore, were doomed; neither made progress.

In Transylvania, Falkenhayn, the old maestro, utilized the wide separation of the Rumanian forces and their dependence upon tenuous supply lines through mountain passes to defeat the enemy in detail. In a succession of battles in late September and early October he first checked and then repulsed the First and Second Rumanian armies. The grand advance into Transylvania quickly became a retreat. At the same time, Mackensen, reinforced with two Turkish divisions, took Constanta, Rumania's only good Black Sea port, and Cernavoda on the Danube and prepared to cross the river and put a pincers on Bucharest, as Falkenhayn drove in from the west and north.

Falkenhayn raced against winter, when the passes would be deep in snow, supply virtually impossible. In a month of hard driving in November, Falkenhayn's Ninth Army crossed the Transylvanian Alps, and forced the Rumanians out of a defensive position along the Aluta River. At the same time Mackensen established a bridgehead across the Danube near Sistova.

It was last gasp for a country that had marched so hopefully to war just two short months before.

But the Rumanians, under General Alexandru Averescu, died trying. A counterattack against Mackensen on December 1 netted prisoners and initial success, only to end in heavy casualties, near panic and quick retreat. The pincers closed on Bucharest on December 6, and Falkenhayn and Mackensen, slowed by heavy rains and mud, pressed the Rumanian remnants, stiffened now by Russians, to the Sereth River, where the campaign petered out in early January, 1917. The Rumanians, avid for glory and for gain, had lost most of their army—300,000 to 400,000 men—and all of their country, except Moldavia in the north. Yet to Germany the victory meant added strain: 60,000 more casualties, and 250 more miles of front to be held with a thin and dwindling line.

MACEDONIA

The Allied troops in the "Entrenched Camp" or so-called "Bird Cage" at Salonika spent the first months of 1916 in construction of roads, piers, and railroads, and in reinforcement. Their position was incongruous politically and militarily. They occupied the soil of Greece, ostensibly a neutral nation. They had no clear-cut directives and London's orders to the five British divisions limited them to an equivocal and essentially static role.

Nevertheless, the force grew in size (by the end of July) to about a quarter of a million men: the British; four French divisions; six reconstituted Serbian divisions; a large Italian division almost the size of a corps, and even a Russian brigade. The French General Maurice Sarrail became titular commander in chief in July after a short Allied advance in March (planned as another diversion, but an ineffective one, to relieve the pressure on Verdun), and a Bulgarian penetration into Greece along the Struma River in May. With the uncertain Greek Army in his rear partially immobilized, partially demobilized, Sarrail established a continuous front in Northern Greece from the Gulf of Orfani to Lake Presba.

Sarrail was ordered to drive north in August to complement Rumania's entry into the war, but the Bulgarian Second Army in the eastern (Struma River) sector attacked first. The Bulgars, however, took their eye off the main chance and occupied territory—the Greek coastal strip of Kavalla—instead of killing Allied soldiers. On September 10 the French and Serbian troops started a limited offensive. In hard fighting over 8,000-foot peaks and up the Monastir Gap they broke through the Bulgarian First Army line and captured Monastir on November 19 after an advance of about twenty-five miles in almost perpendicular country. The Bulgarian First Army was almost finished—a tribute to the ferocious ardor of the renascent Serbs, fighting once again in their own beloved country. The Bulgars were saved by the howling blizzards of a Macedonian winter and by two German divisions, once again hastily scratched together from bits and pieces as far away as France. At Monastir, the offensive stalled, too little and too late to save Rumania. The casualties: 60,000 Bulgars and Germans; 50,000 Allies. The strategic results: nil.

An Italian corps which had been based in southern Albania since 1915 pushed north against Austrian opposition in November, and though operating independently helped to form a more or less continuous front from the Adriatic to the Aegean Sea.

ITALY

Cadorna, who probably practiced the bloody tactics of attrition more than any other general of World War I, started battering again at the stone wall of the Isonzo front in the so-called Fifth Battle of the Isonzo (March 11-29). It was a feckless assault, part of the Allied grand strategy to pin down Austrian divisions, but it made minuscule gains.

Conrad, obsessed by a contemptuous hatred for his Italian foes, started an offensive of his own from the Trentino in May. It was against Falkenhayn's advice and without German support; he had told Conrad that neither the number of troops nor the railroad facilities were adequate to secure a breakthrough. But Conrad transferred some of his best divisions from the Russian front (thereby facilitating Brusilov's later successes) and concentrated some two thousand guns in the Trentino bulge. The preparations could not be kept secret; Cadorna, utilizing his interior lines of communication, commenced transferring troops to the area after ending the Fifth Battle of the Isonzo.

Nevertheless, the Italians failed to prepare deep defenses and on May 15, the Austrian Archduke Eugen's Eleventh and Third armies (fifteen divisions) drove southward in the so-called Asiago offensive, toward the rail junctions of Thiene and Bassano. The battlefield was a mountain labyrinth of rocky peaks, deep gorges, and small valleys; the artillery echoed in shattering reverberations and rock and snow slides obliterated trench lines. Despite the terrain, the Austrians drove a five-mile wedge through the Italian positions and captured thousands of prisoners. But gradually reserves, terrain, and exhaustion slowed the offensive; Falkenhayn had been right.

By June 10, after a twelve-mile gain (in one salient) the attack was halted, never to be resumed, for Brusilov was driving hard in the East. Cadorna began a counterattack in mid-June; by the end of the month the Austrians gave up a large share of their gains and retired to carefully prepared defensive positions. The score card showed huge Italian losses, a minimum of 147,000 casualties of all types (some estimates are twice this number), and the Italian government fell. The Austrians suffered about eighty to one hundred thousand casualties in the Asiago drive, but Conrad's brashness had helped Brusilov to enormous gains.

Cadorna turned once again to the Isonzo, and in the Sixth Battle (August 6-17), with almost a three to one superiority in numbers, he captured the town of Gorizia—the first real fruits of all the Isonzo attempts—and made limited gains in the Carso Plateau. Three more battles followed, with the Italian main efforts directed futilely at the Carso—the Seventh Battle from September 14-26, the Eighth from October 10-12, and the Ninth from November 1-14. As usual throughout Cadorna's regime, the Italians suffered the heavier casualties, and there was mourning in many an Apennine village. But the Austrians, under strain, were being bled white.

THE WAR AT SEA

Admiral Reinhard Scheer, who relieved the ineffective Hugo von Pohl on January 19, commenced a vigorous offensive campaign with submarine, airship, and mine, backed up by the High Seas Fleet. He made numerous sorties in an attempt to force the British to disperse their naval forces and to catch and destroy them in detail. The early months of the year were marked by sea and air raids, counterraids, mining, and desultory clashes between light forces.

In late May British naval intelligence, prewarned by the chattering radios of German U-boats moving into position off British ports, warned Jellicoe at Scapa Flow and Beatty at Rosyth that something "big" was impending. Scheer had sent out his cruisers, steaming north toward the Skagerrak to entice the British battle cruisers within range of the High Seas Fleet. Thus, the stage was set as Beatty and Jellicoe moved eastward across the murky waters of the North Sea for what was to be the greatest naval battle of the war.

The Grand Fleet had a marked superiority to the High Seas Fleet on May 31, 1916, as H.M.S. *Galatea* sighted light cruiser *Elbing* of the Imperial German Navy, and signaled: "Enemy in sight."

Jellicoe counted under his command twenty-eight battle-ships and nine battle cruisers; eight armored cruisers; twenty-six light cruisers; and seventy-eight destroyers and flotilla leaders. Scheer's fleet numbered twenty-two battleships (some obsolescent); five battle cruisers; eleven light cruisers; and sixty-one destroyers and flotilla leaders. Yet Jellicoe was, in Churchill's words, the "only man who could lose the war in an afternoon," and he knew it. In his own words he felt he could not leave "anything to chance in a fleet action, because our fleet was the one and only factor that was vital to the existence of the Empire."

Beatty and Hipper—ahead of the main fleets—opened the ball with their scouting forces. After *Galatea*'s contact, a plane, swung out from H.M.S. *Engadine*, seaplane tender, made history by a scouting flight which sighted German cruisers. The report never reached Beatty, but it was the birth of naval airpower.

The battle was joined at 3:48 P.M. in a sullen afternoon. Steaming hard, the two battle cruiser forces made contact off the Skagerrak. Hipper immediately reversed course to draw Beatty back upon the main body of the High Seas Fleet. Beatty, always aggressive, followed hard, despite the fact that four fast battleships of his command were well out of range astern. The battle opened at ranges varying from 10,000 to 17,000 yards, with the British ships clear against the western skyline, the German ships dull shapes in the mist to the east. Superior German gunnery and defects in the designs of the British battle cruisers quickly told.

By 4 P.M. *Tiger* had been hit, and *Lion*, Beatty's flagship, had received its fourth hit from *Lützow*. Q Turret blew up. Major F. J. W. Harvey of the Royal Marines—both legs severed—ordered the handling room crew to flood the magazines and saved the ship with his dying words. At 4:30 *Indefatigable* disappeared in a terrible sheet of flame and smoke; only two of her crew survived. At 4:06 Sir Hugh Evan-Thomas, with Beatty's four fast battleships, got into the fight at 19,000 yards range, and a 15-inch shell from *Barham* cut through *Von der Tann*'s armor and 600 tons of water flooded into the German ship.

The running fight stood on to the south at twenty-three knots as Hipper led Beatty toward the High Seas Fleet. The *Queen Mary* died at 4:26; a column of smoke mushroomed a thousand feet high and great fluttering clouds of paper, bodies, limbs, turret armor, and a lifeboat were hurled high into the air. Nine men out of 1,275 survived.

Princess Royal took a German salvo and a signalman on *Lion*'s flag bridge mistakenly reported her blown up.

Beatty, imperturbable, turned to his flag captain: "Chatfield, there seems to be something wrong with our bloody ships today. Turn two points to port [toward the Germans]."

At 4:50, as the dusk was coming down soon after Scheer's main battle fleet had been sighted, Beatty reversed course to the north, falling back upon Jellicoe in a running fight. Evan-Thomas's tough battleships brought up the rear and gave as good as they received. By 6 P.M. all of *Von der Tann*'s guns were out of action, her decks a shambles; *Seydlitz* was afire; *Lützow* and *Derfflinger* seriously damaged.

The sun was low before the main fleets met at last about 6:15 P.M. Squarely across Scheers course, capping the T of his column, lay the might and majesty of England—*King George V* and *Ajax; Iron Duke* and *St. Vincent; Temeraire* and *Marlborough; Agincourt* and *Collingwood;* and a host of others bearing proud and ancient names and flying the cross of St. George.

The range was shortened now to 11,000 to 16,000 yards and the British had the advantage of the fading light. At 6:36 Scheer simultaneously reversed the course of his entire fleet—turning southward away from the gaping jaws of the British crescent. But not before he drew blood again; *Invincible*, British battle cruiser, joined the growing company

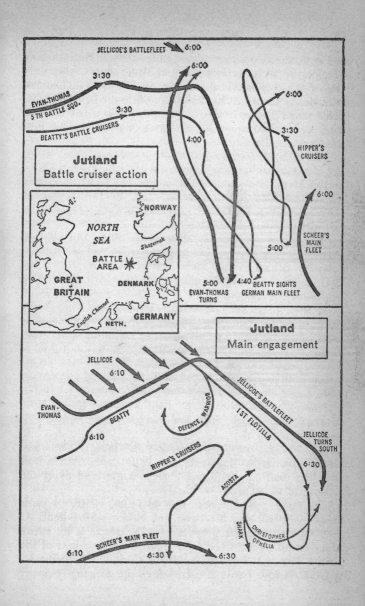

of the departed. Scheer turned north again to the assault at 6:55, partly to try to succor the sinking light cruiser *Wiesbaden* and to aid the crippled *Lützow*. But not for long. His van was the focus for the broadsides of no fewer than thirty-three major British ships. It was too much. Scheer turned again to southward, covering his retirement with a torpedo attack upon the British battleships. Jellicoe, the cautious, turned his battleships *away* from the torpedoes of the retreating Germans and the main fight was over.

The rest was a sprawling, disconnected series of actions all that night until well after dawn of June 1 between the light forces of the two fleets. *Elbing* and *Frauenlob* died in the night action; the *Lützow* sank; the *Pommern* blew up; men struggled and drowned in the cold waters. But the German High Seas Fleet withdrew to safety beyond Horn Reefs and the British Grand Fleet limped home to Scapa and Rosyth to lick its wounds, and mourn its missed opportunity for another Trafalgar.

Jutland, or Skagerrak, as the Germans call it, was undoubtedly a German moral victory; they bearded the world's most powerful fleet in its home waters and inflicted far more injuries than they received. The British lost more than 6,097 men killed or drowned; the Germans, 2,545. Three British battle cruisers, three armored cruisers, and eight destroyers were sunk; the Germans lost one battle cruiser, one old pre-dreadnought battleship, four light cruisers, and five destroyers. Six British ships and four German vessels were seriously damaged.[7]

Jellicoe was overcautious; Beatty overbold; Hipper brilliant. The German gunnery was better, their ships much tougher, than the British. The British lost prestige but retained control of the seas. The two great fleets never clashed again, and two and a half years later the Germans lost the war. In November Jellicoe became First Sea Lord to fight a greater menace than the High Seas Fleet—the submarine. Beatty took command of the Grand Fleet. The strategic importance of the Battle of Jutland was immense. A decisive victory by either side could have altered the course of the war. As it was, the British maintained the crushing power of the distant blockade; the Germans turned more and more to submarine warfare.

The submarine campaign by the time of Jutland had already passed through many vicissitudes and mutations. Within the German government there was a continuous struggle between the advocates of unrestricted submarine warfare, which increased military results (ship sinkings) and the advocates of less political risks. The "sink without notice" policy had softened, hardened, and softened again; finally Moritz von Bethmann-Hollweg, the German Chancellor, warned that the United States would enter the war if submarine operations were not restricted. Alfred von Tirpitz, the able German Navy minister, resigned in March in protest. But even the modified and softened policy led to major incidents: the torpedoing of the French passenger steamer *Sussex* in late March injured a number of Americans and led to a still further, though temporary, restriction on submarine operations.

But indecisive Jutland marked a watershed. To break the British stranglehold the Germans turned more and more toward unrestricted submarine warfare, with all the political risks and moral opprobrium it would imply. The toll of ship sinkings rose steadily in 1916 to 176,000 tons of British vessels sunk in each of the months of the last quarter of the year (the highest toll to date), plus in October 102,000 tons of neutral shipping (also a high record) and almost 75,000 tons of Allied shipping. Total sinkings of all flags averaged 192,-000 tons a month, 79,000 tons more than in 1915.[8] The blockaders were becoming blockaded.

Another indirect result of the Battle of Jutland was the death of Lord Kitchener of Khartoum, British war minister and national hero. A German submarine had laid mines off the Orkneys precedent to the sortie of the High Seas Fleet in late May. Kitchener embarked upon the cruiser *Hampshire* on a mission to Russia and on June 5 the *Hampshire* struck a mine, and sank quickly, in a raging sea, with nearly all aboard. For Kitchener's fame his death was timely. He

had lost power, and, in the Cabinet, prestige; he had mud-
dled too often. World War I was not his war, though he
left as his monument the "new armies" which he had organized and trained.

A net and mine barrage laid across the Strait of Dover
against submarines was raided by a German destroyer force
on October 26. The Germans sank six drifters and a destroyer guarding the nets and damaged two other British
vessels at small cost to themselves.

In the Adriatic the Italian Navy lost two battleships during
the year: one, *Leonardo da Vinci* (August 2) due to sabotage
and fire in the harbor of Taranto; the other, *Regina Marghe-
rita,* by an Italian-laid mine off Taranto. The Italian naval air
service and motor torpedo boats expanded greatly during 1916.

OUTER THEATERS

The year 1916 started with severe Allied reverses in the
outer theaters of the war. The Gallipoli evacuation was
completed in January; on April 29, Townshend, besieged
since early December, 1915, in Kut al Imara in Mesopotamia
by Turkish and Arab forces, surrendered. Some 10,000 men
—mostly of the Indian Army, but including more than 2,000
Englishmen—were taken prisoner; 1,700 others had died,
2,500 had been wounded during the five-month siege. It had
been an epic of defeat; the men, decimated by disease, had
been on short rations for weeks, but as always in defeats,
there had been mismanagement, poor leadership, little strategic vision. And the epic was tarnished by a last-minute
attempt by the British government to raise the siege by
offering the Turks a two-million-pound ransom.[9] The futile
attempts to relieve Kut, which started in January under
General Fenton Aylmer and continued through April under
General George Gorringe, cost the British almost 22,000
casualties—double the strength of the Kut garrison.

For most of the rest of 1916, Mesopotamia was quiescent,
as the British built up their strength and their supplies. In
August a general named Sir Stanley Maude assumed command, and at last man and opportunity had met. In Decem-

ber, just before the rains came, he started once again—with a superiority over the Turks of more than two to one—a drive to the north toward the magic city of Baghdad.

On the Caucasus front, an able Russian general, Nikolai Yudenich, implementing the strategy of the governor general, the Grand Duke Nicholas, initiated a winter campaign in January, 1916, before the Turks could be reinforced from Gallipoli. The Russians quickly made a fifty-mile gain and captured Erzerum (February 16) and later Trebizond (April 18). By July 25, after numerous halts for regrouping and supply, the Russians reached Erzingian on the edge of the hill country. The rest of the year was squandered in indecisive attack and riposte against the Turkish Second and Third armies.

In the meantime a small Russian force (about 20,000 men) under General N. N. Baratov, supplied via the Caspian Sea, took Hamadan in January, Karind in March, and advanced on Baghdad from the north and east. The threat was an effective diversion; the Turkish Sixth Army withdrew a corps from Kut al Imara, facing the British, to hold the Russians in check. The Turks repulsed a Russian attack at Khanikin on June 1 and that was the virtual end of Russian operations in Persia.

Meanwhile in the Suez Canal-Palestine area, raid and counterraid, buildup and construction featured most of 1916. General Sir Archibald Murray assumed command in Egypt in March, 1916; the maximum force there of fourteen divisions was rapidly reduced, however, to four. The British, toiling with intensity, had built another fortified area near the canal, a strategic answer and a needlessly expensive one to the Turkish attack on the canal in 1915. Then, painstakingly, the British forces started to clear the Sinai peninsula of the enemy, a task which had to be preceded and accompanied by immense logistic efforts, including the laying of water pipelines, and the construction of a railway and a road.

But the Germans and Turks were not dismayed. In the caldron of the desert summer, Kress von Kressenstein led

15,000 Turks and Germans across Sinai to Romani near the seacoast. Murray fought a skillful defensive battle (August 3-4) and repulsed the enemy handily, but the Turks made good their retreat.

An Arab revolt against the Turks began in June in Saudi Arabia; on June 9 the Arabs captured Mecca and in September, Taif.

By year's end, the British had crossed the shifting sands of Sinai, complete with their pipeline, railroad, and road, and had taken El Arish, evacuated by the Turks, and on December 23, Magdhaba, with most of its 1,300-man garrison. The British defense of the Suez Canal now stood on its "natural" frontiers—at the eastern borders of the Sinai peninsula.

In East Africa General Jan Smuts, the grand old man of South Africa, assumed command of all British forces, about 20,000 strong. Beleaguered Lettow-Vorbeck was now squeezed by half a dozen pincers—from the sea, from British East Africa, from Uganda, from the Belgian Congo, and from northern Rhodesia. But he had reached peak strength of about 15,000, including 3,500 Germans, and he received ammunition replenishment from a German blockade runner. Smuts personally led the main effort in the north. The campaign was a succession of outflanking movements, of short advances and retreats, skirmishes, and attempts to pin down the superbly handled German forces. Lettow-Vorbeck was constantly backpedaling, but he, personally, was never pinned down.

The campaign was a plodding advance against time and sickness; East Africa was no place for the white man. By year's end the British controlled the main lines of communication in northern and central German East Africa; they had captured the seaport of Dar es Salaam and most of the coastal region and Lettow-Vorbeck and most of his followers were forced south to the Rufiji River area. There had been no great battles, except against disease; each time the British were poised to deliver the decisive blow the German forces broke up into small groups and scattered in the bush to meet and fight another day.

Nineteen-sixteen was a year of disaster for both sides, of great deeds unrequited by any obvious gain, of strategy stultified by the machine gun and the trench and the out-worn ideas of other wars. The war's insatiable demands for-ever grew. Germany passed a compulsory employment law governing every male from seventeen to sixty. The air raids increased; nine Zeppelins attempted to raid Liverpool on January 31, 1916. And seaplanes and land planes in small numbers joined the attacks. Britain concentrated twelve fighter squadrons and perhaps five hundred antiaircraft guns for the defense but the raids continued, and morale suffered. The mighty fell in 1916; Joffre and Kitchener and Tirpitz and Falkenhayn, and toward the end of the year, Prime Minister Asquith of Britain. The British war effort had lacked coordination. The Sinn Fein Easter Week rebellion in Ireland ruthlessly repressed, the Jutland battle, the terri-ble failure of the Somme, the fall of Kut, and above all, the growing sense of hopeless horror at the unavailing slaughter, contributed to Asquith's fall. But so did David Lloyd George, the fiery, demagogic, unpredictable Welshman, with ambition unlimited, who undercut his chief. Lloyd George took office, with boundless energy, far-ranging ideas, and a fixed opinion that Haig and the "Colonel Blimps" of the British Army did not know how to run the war. His powerful but erratic personality was to make increasing impact upon the war—and the peace.

In the United States, just emerging from its golden age to an era of income taxes and preparedness, Woodrow Wilson barely captured a second term as President, with his sup-porters boasting: "He kept us out of war."

A smash hit was the popular song: "I Didn't Raise My Boy to Be a Soldier."

A few understood; the Plattsburgh training camps were starting, and some modern Minute Men drilled with broom-sticks.

And in Switzerland a man named N. Lenin[10] waited, biding his time.

V

THE FATEFUL YEAR—1917

NINETEEN-SEVENTEEN was a year that history will long mark well. The United States forswore the advice of George Washington against entangling alliances and joined upon a "war to end war," and a "crusade to make the world safe for Democracy." In Russia, "out of the gutters and ghettoes of Eastern Europe," there rose to power a national revolution and international conspiracy. Its mordant effects still sway the world almost half a century later. War propaganda —"foul whisperings are abroad"—fanned the flames of emotion. Some of it was true, most false. But, verily, the fiction-mongers could not match the real enormity of slaughter. And the war became bigger, and ever bigger; British artillery in France increased from 749 guns and 882 howitzers of all calibers on January 1, 1915, to 3,433 guns and 1,574 howitzers on January 1, 1917.[1]

THE WESTERN FRONT

The Allied plans for 1917 contemplated "decisive" and nearly simultaneous attacks on the three main fronts—in the West, in the East, and in Italy. As usual, "the best laid schemes o' mice and men/Gang aft a-gley," and events super-seded hopes. Germany, her armies feeling the strain of a multifront war and weakened by the Somme, was outnumbered in the West in January, 1917; almost four million Allied soldiers faced two and a half million Germans. German plans contemplated, therefore, a defensive in the West, unrestricted submarine warfare at sea, and aid to Austria against Italy.

General Nivelle, the ebullient boaster who succeeded Joffre, sold himself to the French government on the basis of a ruthless and violent offensive. He planned a great "blow of a gigantic fist"[2] against the flanks of the same salient— the huge Noyon bulge—that the Allies had been trying to reduce for three years. But again, the Germans moved first.

This time—in retreat, not attack. From February 25 to April 5, under Ludendorff's skillful direction, the German armies conducted a staged withdrawal from the Noyon bulge to a series of much shorter prepared positions, known as the Hindenburg Line (the Germans called it the Siegfried Line). The maximum withdrawal was more than thirty-one miles, the greatest movement in the West in three years of war. The new positions, seamed with field fortifications in depth, were extremely strong, and the shortened line could be held with some thirteen fewer divisions. Thus, the retirement helped to meet Germany's greatest need—reserves. Behind them, in the abandoned salient they had held so long, the Germans left "scorched earth." Wells were poisoned; wreckage booby-trapped; villages, roads, trees, and railroads obliterated; there was no sign of human life—only a vast wilderness. The Allies had to build as they followed the retreating foe.

But bumptious Nivelle—one of history's best examples of the influence of the persuasive personality upon politicians— was not dismayed. His attack became bigger and better; he distributed plans and orders far and wide; he even talked openly to the ladies about the forthcoming battle at a London dinner party. Before long, the Germans knew as much about what was impending as Nivelle did.

The British started 1917's gruesome campaigns on a terrible Easter morning, April 9, with an attack at Arras, where the Hindenburg Line's northwestern flank was anchored on

Vimy Ridge. From April 9 to 24 on a fourteen-mile front, Sir Edmund Allenby's Third Army and a Canadian corps (twelve divisions in the initial assault) drove hard against strong enemy resistance. Haig's answer to prior failures was more artillery; the preparatory bombardment lasted a week and during the battle about 88,000 tons of artillery and ammunition were expended. New contact fuses and new projectors for gas helped the attackers. Air superiority ultimately won by the British after spectacular sky battles with Richtofen's "circus" helped. The Canadians took and held Vimy Ridge, a dominating *terrain massif*, and this was an achievement of consequence a year later. But Arras in 1917 was again a limited victory—a two- to five-mile advance on a twenty-mile front, 18,128 Germans and 230 guns captured, 57,000 other enemy casualties at the cost of some 84,000 British casualties.[3]

Nivelle's great main effort by the French Fifth, Sixth, Tenth, and First armies (about fifty-four divisions, including fourteen in reserve) was launched April 16, while the guns were still thundering at Arras. The Second Battle of the Aisne was fought on a fifty-mile front from Soissons to Rheims. The terrain, including the 650-foot eminence of the Chemin des Dames, and the Craonne plateau, seamed with ravines, had been turned into a "veritable fortress" by the Germans—"one of the strongest positions in Europe."[4]

Nivelle laid on an eleven-million-shell bombardment and radiated confidence—but not for long. The much advertised "end-the-war breakthrough" ground to a dead halt on the first day. The French ultimately captured the commanding terrain feature, the Chemin des Dames, and pushed a few shallow bulges into the German lines. But by late May when the battle died out, the French had lost about 120,000 men.

Nivelle with his bombast was finished; Pétain, the "Savior of Verdun," assumed command. The Second Aisne, plus Nivelle, were the straws that broke the camel's back. The French Army mutinied—probably the largest mutinies in a great army in modern history. The futile bloodletting, the endless fighting, insufficient leave, poor recreational facilities, too great a gulf between officers and men, antiwar strikes, agitation and despair on the home front, German propaganda, and the virus of the Russian Revolution all played a part. Whole divisions refused duty.

> Camps were placarded with notices declaring the intention of the soldiers to refuse to go back again to the trenches. . . . A battalion ordered to the front . . . dispersed in a wood. Soldiers coming home on leave sang the Internationale in the trains and demanded peace. Mutinies occurred in sixteen different Army Corps. . . . A number of young infantrymen marched through the streets of a French town, "baa-ing" like sheep to indicate they were being driven like lambs to the slaughter.[5]

Two Russian brigades that had been serving with the French were badly handled in the fighting, and suffered heavily. They gave the most trouble; artillery fire had to be turned against them. The sullen survivors included one Sergeant R. Y. Malinovsky, who was to become a marshal of the Red Army in another war a generation later.[6]

For Henri Philippe Pétain, this was his finest hour. Pétain had a feel for the *poilu;* known as the soldiers' champion, he commanded their respect. Pétain was indefatigable; he personally visited some ninety divisions in his first month in command—listening to the complaints of the men, exhorting the officers, arranging for more leaves, better recreation and better food, and stressing leadership.

In the end, investigations and courts-martial finished, some semblance of discipline restored, some fifty-five ringleaders[7] were executed and France went on with the war.

But cautiously, and committed for the rest of 1917 to slow recovery. Pétain knew that the French Army must have rest and recuperation; he told the British they must shoulder the main burden on the Western Front while the Allies waited for American manpower to help turn the tide.

This was a large order. For by now the strategic situation in the West which had seemed favorable to the Allies at the beginning of the year was reversed. The Russian Revolution had freed German troops for the Western Front; Italy, overwhelmed by disaster, needed help; and the French divisions could man only the quiet sectors of the long line from Switzerland to the sea. But the mutinies were kept secret; the Germans never learned until too late of the desperate condition of France.

So the British took up the burden. Haig had indeed planned an offensive in Flanders for some time—long before the French mutinies occurred. The mutinies seemed an added reason to draw German forces to the British front, and British intelligence had supplied glowingly optimistic estimates of German weaknesses and raddled morale. The infamous Ypres salient—the British Tommy called it "Wipers"—was selected once again for the scene of a major battle, and the Belgian Channel ports loomed, like a glittering mirage, as the prize of victory.

Haig put in a limited objective attack against Messines Ridge, which commanded the Ypres salient, on June 7, to protect the southern flank of his main effort.

Sir Herbert Plumer's Second Army conducted a carefully prepared assault on a nine-mile front. It was preceded by some seventeen days of intense bombardment, assisted and directed by British aircraft. Since early 1916, the British had been tunneling toward Messines, and the Germans had been driving countermines, or saps, toward the British works. This battle in the dark, scores to hundreds of feet beneath the shell-scarred surface, had sometimes led to hand-to-hand struggles in the tunnels, with men clawing at each other's throats and beating each other to death with picks and shovels.[8]

But at Messines, the British won beneath the ground, on the ground, and in the air. Nineteen mines with some 500 tons of explosives were detonated simultaneously beneath the German positions at zero hour—0310 June 7—and an awful barrage followed. A few stunned Germans were left alive. German reserves moved in later to fill the gap and the British got some stiff fighting, but the Messines Ridge was taken before nightfall and the southern flank of the Ypres salient was secure. And for the first time, the German defensive casualties were slightly larger than the attacking British casualties.

The Third Battle of Ypres, one of the bloodiest of the war, started in late July after long preparations. Messines had warned the Germans; they had formed reserves and strengthened their lines. More important, the Flanders plain was a bog, a hog wallow, with mud deep enough to drown men and beasts. The drainage ditches and canals had been broken down by the incessant flogging of the shells, and in three years of war the once fertile farmlands had been turned into a nightmare landscape ". . . a fluid clay . . . a treacherous slime."

A steady drenching rain set in on the day of the infantry assault (July 31) and as the skies dripped for days on end:

> . . . men staggered wearily over duckboard tracks. Wounded men falling headlong into the shell holes were in danger of drowning. Mules slipped from the tracks and were often drowned in the giant shell holes along side. Guns sank till they became useless; rifles caked and would not fire; even food was tainted with the inevitable mud.[9]

The Fifth Army, with some eighteen divisions, nevertheless attacked again and again, its flanks protected by the British Second Army and the French First Army.

It was a long and grim ordeal, its horror forever etched on the minds and hearts of those who fought there. For the first time the Germans used a blistering, burning chemical called "mustard gas," which mixed with the mud and water to cause, long after its release, persistent casualties. And German aircraft strafed the toiling British Tommies from the air. At last, on November 6, as the grim winter was closing down, the Canadians took Passchendaele Ridge. But the front was still unbroken; the Ypres salient was deepened but not widened, and the British had lost at least 245,000 men, more probably 380,000—almost double the German losses. But the latter were losses Germany could ill afford.[10]

Pétain, nursing the French Army back to health, launched two small-scale limited objective offensives in the late summer and fall, to help restore French combat self-confidence. Both were very carefully prepared and strictly limited; both were small successes. At Verdun from August 20-26 the French Second Army, with twelve divisions, took the high ground overlooking Verdun, captured 10,000 prisoners, and sustained small losses. At Malmaison on the Aisne, the French Tenth Army attacked with eight divisions on a ten-mile front from October 23 to November 2, and with the help of tanks, surprise, and carefully rehearsed coordination between all arms, eliminated the Soissons salient and seized all the heights of the Aisne.

In November, Georges Benjamin Eugene Clemenceau— "The Tiger"—succeeded Paul Painlevé as Premier of France. His fierce courage and redoubtable energy were to pilot France to victory.

And then, at Cambrai from November 20 to December 7, the British tried again, with new and revolutionary tactics.

At Cambrai the tank came of age. At last its technology and tactics had been perfected; at last it was used in mass, not in penny packets; at last, the "tankers" had been able to select their ground and to influence the planning of the battle.

General Julian Byng, commanding the British Third Army, with about twelve divisions (but only five in the initial attack on a six-mile front) and 324 tanks started the surprise assault against a section of the Hindenburg Line on November 20. The tanks were covered by smoke, closely supported by infantry, and carried their own trench-bridging equipment—huge bundles of fascines, or brush. By nightfall the British had penetrated all except the last of the German lines of resistance; and had punched a deep—but irregular— bulge in the German lines toward Cambrai. About 179 tanks were out of action, but only sixty-five due to German fire; the rest were broken down or bogged down. After fierce fighting for Bourlon Wood, a heavy and surprise German counterattack on November 30 won back a large part of the British gains.[11]

Thus, the first rejoicing about Cambrai proved premature;

the British opportunity—about a four-mile gain in one day, as much as was gained at Third Ypres in a hundred days— was squandered because of lack of tank and infantry reserves. But the tank had at last showed its real potential; the lessons were not lost in 1918, and in another war to come.

THE END IN RUSSIA

Grigori Rasputin (literally, the "vagabond") was a lascivious intriguer in the heart of the Czarist court. His influence upon the Czarina, attributable in part to his alleged psychic healing powers, which he applied to the Czar's young son who was afflicted with hemophilia, extended to other members of the court. Whether pro-German or not, Rasputin was a malevolent factor in Petrograd, but a symptom, rather than a cause, of the deadly sickness of the Romanov dynasty. Rasputin's assassination, in December, 1916, merely lanced one boil; the festering illness was not touched. Indeed, the monk's death at the hands of court noblemen increased the tension, already emphasized by harsh criticism in the Duma.

Food shortages, terrible casualty lists, and the Czar's stubborn refusal to liberalize his government led to increasing demonstrations and strikes in the early months of 1917. Petrograd (formerly St. Petersburg, later Leningrad) then the capital of Russia, was seething. Finally, on March 11 (Gregorian style; February 26, old style) the Duma disobeyed the Czar's order of dissolution; a guard regiment murdered its officers; huge fires lit the streets. The prisons were opened; street fighting followed; the revolt spread to Moscow; and at 3 P.M. on March 15, the Czar, at army headquarters in Pskov, abdicated. "May God help Russia," was his prayer and epitaph. A day later, the Grand Duke, the Czar's brother, refused the crown; in a few days the Czar and his family were arrested, and the rule of the house of Romanov was forever ended.

. . . it was not a contrived revolution. No one planned it. No one organized it. Even the Bolsheviki, who for years had dreamed of such a day and had conceived of themselves as professionals in the art of producing revolutions, were taken wholly by surprise. The February revolution was simply the sudden, crashing breakdown of an old dynastic-imperial system, caught between the stresses of a major modern war for which it was inadequate, and the inertia of an imperial court that had lost its orderliness of procedure, its feel for events, its contact with the people, and even the respect of the ruling bureaucracy.[12]

The revolution quickly became a struggle for power between the relatively moderate liberals of the Duma's executive committee, and the Workers' and Soldiers' Councils, or Soviets, established by the Socialists. Out of this struggle a man named Alexander Kerensky, "a lawyer of outstanding rhetorical gifts,"[13] emerged as the leader of the moderate Socialists, and of a provisional government.

But not for long. N. Lenin, who had been in exile for eleven years, was permitted by the Germans to transit Germany from Switzerland in a sealed railroad car. He was joined in Russia by Leon Trotsky (Lev Davidovich Bronstein) who until March 27 had been in New York, and Josef Stalin. The great conspiracy was launched, and the Germans who encouraged it doomed their country in another war.

Kerensky, first as minister of war and navy, then as Prime Minister, with Brusilov as his commander in chief, heeded the pressure of the Allies, and launched the so-called Kerensky offensive in Galicia in July.

It was a ragged hope. Workers' and Soldiers' Councils had been formed in army units; Kerensky himself had provided for the appointment of commissars; discipline had broken down; millions had deserted.

The offensive was launched, however, by the best and least affected units, including many Siberians and Finns, and it made initial progress. The Russian Eleventh, Seventh, and Eighth armies, with more than forty attenuated divisions, drove toward Lemberg and Halicz. The opposing forces were a polyglot of many nations and races—the exhausted Austrians, and some German and Turkish divisions. As usual, against the Germans, the Russians did not do too well, but General Lavr Kornilov's Eighth Army in the south, operating against the Austrians, made about a twenty-mile advance; Rumanians and Russians on their flank also made some gains. It was a short-lived triumph.

The Central Powers, aided by a few divisions transferred from the West, launched a counteroffensive on July 19, and the Russian front virtually dissolved. Entire units deserted; within a few days, there was little serious fighting and the Germans and Austrians advanced as they pleased. Before year's end, they had cleared Galicia of the remnants of the gigantic "steam roller" which, so hopefully, three years before, had moved ponderously to war.

In the North, as a prod to Kerensky to talk peace, the German Eighth Army (Oskar von Hutier) crossed the Dvina River and captured Riga on September 3, against inconsequential resistance. The tactics were more notable than the victory; Hutier used surprise, night marches, a short heavy artillery preparation, a rolling barrage, infiltration, mobility. The Germans sent an amphibious expedition to capture Riga's offshore islands as a threat to Petrograd.

Doom was not long deferred. In the so-called October Revolution (November 7-8, new-style calendar) what remained of the old Russia went down to defeat, not with a bang but a whimper. The Bolsheviks headed by Lenin and Trotsky seized power; the Winter Palace in Petrograd, site of the legitimate government, was defended only by a unit of women soldiers and a few officers. Kerensky escaped; the moderate Socialists who had supported liberalism but not tyranny walked out of the government, with Trotsky screaming: "Your role is played out. Go where you belong from now on—into the rubbish can of history."[14]

The revolution spread rapidly, Russia was in chaos, civil war started. But there was now no turning back; Trotsky had been right. A small party that originally numbered no more than 80,000 people imposed its will upon the greatest national land mass on earth.

The Bolsheviks quickly initiated discussions to take Russia

out of the war, thus freeing for the first time since 1914 thousands of German troops for duty in the West. The Rumanians followed suit. Armistice terms providing for a month's truce were signed December 15, and Russian, German, Austro-Hungarian, Bulgarian, and Turkish delegations met in Brest-Litovsk on December 22 to arrange permanent peace terms. The Russians were balky, but the Germans knew they had the upper hand. Baron Richard von Kuhlmann, German foreign minister (August, 1917-July, 1918) and head of delegations of the Central Powers, was coldly cynical: "The only choice they have," he said of the Russians, "is as to what sort of sauce they shall be eaten with."[15]

THE UNITED STATES ENTERS THE WAR

The slow drift of the United States toward war had been marked, ever since 1915, by the increasingly sharp tone of the diplomatic correspondence between Washington and Berlin.

In 1914, United States neutrality was undoubtedly supported by the great majority of the American people, though a majority was probably also predisposed in sympathy toward the Allies. But in three years of war, a combination of factors had slowly altered public opinion.

The German violation of Belgian neutrality turned many Americans against Berlin. The militarism and haughty arrogance of the Prussian Junker class, which seemed to the average American to be epitomized by the Kaiser, antagonized others. There was, too, the natural American sympathy for the underdog, and France, the invaded, appeared the underdog. Then, too, there were more English and French sympathizers in the northeastern part of the United States than German, and it was the Northeast—from Boston to Washington—which dominated the most important newspapers and communications media. Britain controlled the global network of cables, and did not hesitate to use her control as an implement of war. German stupidity and British skill in the propaganda field also contributed to the change in American public opinion.

Propaganda, indeed, had much to do—overtly and subtly —with altering men's minds. The British, partly because of their favorable communications position and common language, had all the best of this battle. The German execution in 1915 in Belgium of Edith Cavell, a British nurse convicted of aiding Allied soldiers to escape, aroused intense emotion. The story lost nothing in the British telling of it, and it blanketed the world. On the other hand few Americans ever knew that the French executed nine women as spies during the war, including the glamorous Mata Hari, and the plain Marguerite Schmidt, who died, along with Nurse Cavell, in 1915. Many alleged German atrocities were dignified and given verisimilitude by being included in a supposedly thorough report by Lord Bryce.

The stories of the "crucified Canadians," the "handless babies," the raped women with breasts cut off, cropped up again and again in varied forms and places, though there was little or no evidence to sustain them. To half a world, the Germans became the "Hun" and the "Boche."[16]

German stupidity hurt their own cause. Their clumsy attempts at propaganda in the United States backfired; and the undercover activities of Captain Carl von Boy-Ed, the German naval attaché in Washington, led to his recall and much resentment. Sabotage efforts angered the nation. The crowning stupidity was the so-called Zimmermann note in February, 1917. This note from the German foreign secretary (1916-17) to the German minister in Mexico was intercepted and decoded by the British, who lost no time in letting the Americans know about it. Zimmermann proposed that if the United States entered the war against Germany, Mexico should make war on the United States; its reward, "the lost territory in Texas, New Mexico, and Arizona."[17]

Thus, gradually but definitely, emotions were engaged, minds challenged; like water dripping upon rock, neutralism was worn away.

German unrestricted submarine warfare was unquestionably the greatest factor in the process. There had been friction with Britain in the early years of the war about her surface blockade of Germany; Americans resented interference with their shipping on the high seas. But German submarine warfare was conducted at the expense of American lives, and it became more and more ruthless. The *Lusitania,* sunk in 1915, was never forgotten. But it was followed by incident after incident. In answer to the sharp tone of American protests Germany restricted her U-boats from time to time, only to return to what the British liked to call the policy of *Schrecklichkeit* (frightfulness). The die was cast when Berlin's strategy for 1917 committed Germany to the defensive in the West, but to an unrestricted submarine offensive (within a specified war zone around the British Isles and Allied Europe) against the shipping of all nations. The unrestricted warfare started February 1, 1917, and soon there were more American civilian deaths on the high seas.

Freedom of the seas had long been one of the primary freedoms to Americans; the German challenge led directly to war.

Then, too, there were some few who foresaw America's future role as a world power. To them, failure to participate in the European war, failure to tip the scales against a German autocratic hegemony in Europe, would mean not only loss of trade, but the relative reduction of the United States in the scale of nations. And the Russian Revolution, which overthrew a monarchical autocracy, eased the consciences of those who viewed the war as a struggle for democracy.

And so, in early 1917, the United States drew ever closer to the brink. Woodrow Wilson broke diplomatic relations with Germany, armed merchantmen, and finally after a terrible personal struggle, the President asked Congress in early April to declare war upon Germany. On April 6 the United States joined the war. Thus, the President who only five months before had won a close election on the platform "he kept us out of war" became an apostle of "force, force to the utmost, force without stint or limit." And yet it was more Germany's doing than it was Washington's; Berlin had deliberately accepted the risks when it embarked upon unrestricted submarine warfare; it believed United States armed power would be little and late.

And Berlin had good reason to think so. The United States Regular Army plus the Federalized National Guard, which had been mobilized on the Mexican border, numbered 208,034. There were an additional 101,174 Guardsmen still in state service. There was not a single complete division. The navy, far more ready, had barely started a major construction program in 1916. Some American factories were tooled up manufacturing weapons or equipment for the Allies, but the United States was scarcely an arsenal of democracy.

America's air forces—then organized as the aviation section of the Army Signal Corps—numbered some 130 pilots and 55 obsolescent planes, plus a few pilots and planes in the Naval Air Service.

But West Point and Annapolis had provided a hard core of able professional officers, and the Plattsburgh training camps, initiated as a preparedness measure prior to United States entry, had added additional "citizen-officers." There was a crusading spirit in the land, and soon "The Yanks Are Coming" was echoing over every town and city in the forty-eight states.

For the first time, the United States invoked the draft, or conscription, almost from the beginning of conflict; it was passed on May 19, and by fall the first of more than three million draftees were donning uniforms. (In all, including volunteers, four million men were to serve in the army; 800,000 more in the navy.) In answer to Allied suggestions that the quick appearance of even a small token force of American troops in Europe would help morale, the 1st Division was formed out of scattered Regular Army units, and major elements plus a marine regiment reached France in June, 1917. It was preceded by the junior major general on the army list, Major General John J. ("Black Jack") Pershing, who was selected, in part because of his performance in chasing the bandit "Pancho" Villa in Mexico, to

head the American Expeditionary Force. Pershing set the
tone immediately; this was to be an American army under
American command, and the divisions were to be big—
almost 28,000 men, approximately twice as large as the
British and French units.

From June on, there was a steady flow of green American
units to Europe: the rest of the 1st Division; the units
which ultimately comprised the 2nd; the 26th (Yankee) National Guard Division; the Rainbow Division (the 42nd)
from all over the country.

Pershing set up headquarters at Chaumont; American
dumps and supply bases sprouted all over France and, in
late October, units of the 1st Division moved into a quiet
sector of the French front near Nancy, where on October 23,
at five minutes past six in the morning, American troops
fired their first shots of the war in anger. In early November
three American soldiers were killed by the Germans in a
trench raid—the first of thousands to die—and 2,500 Americans, medical attachments and engineer units, participated
in supporting roles with the British in the Cambrai battle.
By the end of 1917 about 50,000 men a month were being
transported from four Canadian and six United States ports
to six French and many British ports. The Yanks were coming, and just in time.

Back home, the nation was mobilizing—its men, its factories, its resources. Never before had the United States attempted to do so much so quickly; training camps grew
out of farmlands and forests all over the nation; factories
worked three shifts; the shipyards were booming. The nation—so short a time before turned inward upon itself—
looked now to the world; the youthful muscles it was flexing
for the first time were those of the most powerful country
on earth.

THE WAR AT SEA

The United States Navy, which numbered only 73,000
officers and men in April, 1917, was able to intervene almost

immediately—though in modest strength—in the war at sea. Its aid was badly needed.

Admiral William S. Sims, Commander-in-Chief, United States Naval Forces, Europe, called on Admiral John Jellicoe, First Sea Lord, in London on April 10. He learned that German submarines had sunk 1,300,000 tons of Allied and neutral shipping in the first three months of 1917. April's losses, it was estimated, would total almost 900,000 tons.[18] ". . . it is impossible for us to go on with the war if losses like this continue," Jellicoe said.[19]

Jellicoe added that no solution was in sight. The German unrestricted submarine campaign was launched on February 1, with about 111 U-boats in commission. Something like 21,500,000 tons of shipping were available to the Allies; a minimum of 15,500,000 tons, it was estimated, was needed to continue the war. About one-third of the six-million-ton "cushion" had been sunk when Sims arrived in London. Shipyards were producing replacements far too slowly to compensate for the losses. By October, 1917, the end would be in sight; available shipping would total less, if the sinkings continued, than the 15,500,000 tons required.[20]

The problem was a Jules Verne nightmare; command of the sea had hitherto always belonged to the navy that could control its surface. Now the U-boats, operating beneath the sea, were severing Britain's maritime arteries.

In late April Admiral Sims reported:

> Allies do not now command the sea. Transport of troops and supplies strained to the utmost and the maintenance of the armies in the field is threatened.[21]

Until Sims reached London, the conventional remedies—mining of the submarines' home waters, arming of merchantmen, "Q" or decoy ships, smoke screens, and the establishment of patrolled routes along the shipping bottlenecks to the British Isles—had been tried and found wanting.

Sims, Admiral Beatty, and Prime Minister Lloyd George believed more drastic steps were needed. They threw their influence behind Commander Reginald Henderson and a small group in the Admiralty who favored the marshaling of merchant ships into convoys and the protection of the convoys during transit by warships. It was a simple idea, but it was to win the war.

There were already some precedents for the convoy system. Coal convoys between England and France started in March; Scandinavian convoys were initiated in April, and the first transatlantic convoy from New York sailed in May. Throughout the rest of the year the convoy system was steadily expanded and extended with amazing success. By November 30, only eleven ships out of a total of 1,280 in the New York to England convoys had been lost (though heavy losses were suffered in the Scandinavian convoys late in the year from German surface raiders). Total ship sinkings showed a steady decline in the last half of the year, despite the fact that the Germans had 140 U-boats in commission in October, 1917—the peak of the entire war. At the same time United States shipyards joined the British in a massive program of replacements. There is no doubt that the conferences and decisions following Admiral Sims's arrival in London in April, 1917, represented the turning point in the war against the submarine. By December, total sinkings were less than 400,000 tons; never again did the losses approach the peak figure of 881,000 tons sunk in April, 1917.[22]

The most immediate and important United States naval contribution to the war at sea was the strengthening of British antisubmarine forces. On May 4, six ships of a United States destroyer division under Captain J. K. Taussig reached Queenstown, Ireland, a key base where the transoceanic maritime routes funneled into the British Isles. Captain Taussig reported immediately upon arrival to a British admiral for duty and was asked: "At what time will your vessels be ready for sea?" Taussig's answer was simple: "I shall be ready when fueled."[23]

By August 1, the United States had based in European waters thirty-seven destroyers, two tenders, and eight converted yachts—a force which was to grow steadily in size, variety, and effectiveness. In December, the British Grand Fleet, which had lost one of its battleships, the *Vanguard*, from an explosion of undetermined origin in Scapa Flow (July 9), was reinforced by the 6th Battle Squadron, composed of the United States battleships *New York*, *Arkansas*, *Wyoming*, *Florida*, and *Delaware* (subsequently joined in February, 1918, by a sixth ship, the *Texas*). Three other United States battleships were based in Ireland as a convoy support force against surface raiders.

Nineteen-seventeen was also marked by a series of coastal raids by both sides and clashes between light forces. The Germans made numerous forays against the Dover barrage— a barrier of nets and mines across the Strait of Dover guarded by drifters and a destroyer patrol. On April 20, British flotilla leaders *Broke* and *Swift* intercepted German destroyers, based on Zeebrugge. The melee—gunfire, torpedoes, and ramming—ended in a brief hand-to-hand action; two German destroyers were sunk and *Broke* and *Swift* badly damaged.

In May a historic forecast of the future was the torpedoing and sinking of a British merchantman by a German seaplane —the first successful use of this weapon in war.

Mines were laid with profligacy by both sides and most of the Western ocean, including the entire North Sea-Strait of Dover-English Channel area became a zone of peril.

There was one brief clash of major forces, on November 17, in Heligoland Bight as elements of the Grand Fleet caught German small craft sweeping for mines. The German sweepers were supported by heavy ships, and again the British came out second best. The British scored six hits on the Germans, but with minor effect; the Germans lost twenty-one killed and forty wounded. The British suffered one hundred casualties and some bad damage.

But the days of glory of the German High Seas Fleet had ended. Both in the Jade and the Adriatic the virus of revolution, nurtured by war weariness and the moral effect of United States belligerency, caused naval mutinies. The Austrian fleet, long immured in the Adriatic, was affected first. On February 1 in the port of Cattaro the red flag was hoisted on some ships, and a shore battery fired on the *Erzherzog Rudolph*. In two days the mutiny was crushed, but the virus still lived. In May, the High Seas Fleet was affected, and in August there was open disobedience in *Prinzregent Luitpold* and *Friedrich der Grosse*. Two ringleaders were executed, the mutiny was crushed, but again the virus lived.

In the waning days of the year Admiral Jellicoe—frayed by anxiety, worn by burdens—was relieved as First Sea Lord by Admiral Sir Rosslyn Wemyss.

The Italian Front

The fortunes of Conrad, Austria's greatest soldier, waned with the old Emperor's death. In February, he was relieved by the Emperor Carl—Franz Josef's successor—but was assigned a field command on the Trentino front.

The Russian Revolution permitted Austrian reinforcement of the Italian front, but nevertheless Cadorna, responsive to the Allied plans which had envisaged an offensive in Italy, resumed his battering in the Isonzo sector. In the Tenth Battle of the Isonzo (May 12-June 8), the Italians captured some mountain positions, and made gains in the Carso plateau—a limited success at heavy cost. More important, elements of the Italian Third Army surrendered in droves, infected by the same virus that had spread like wildfire from Petrograd throughout the world.

Cadorna returned to the attack in the Eleventh Battle of the Isonzo (August 18-September 15) with a two-to-one local superiority. The attack in the Carso sector was easily fended off by the Austrians, but the Italian Second Army, on the northern flank of a forty-five-mile front, drove a six-mile bulge into the Austrian positions and captured most of the Bainsizza plateau. Exhausted, suffering from heavy losses, and racked by subversive propaganda, the Italians stalled just short of a breakthrough.

The Germans were alarmed. One more blow and perhaps

the entire Austrian front would collapse. Stiffening was needed—and provided.

The German concentrations were detected by the Italians along the Isonzo front; the thunderbolt was not unexpected. But as in the Trentino the year before, orders to prepare defensive positions in depth had been ignored. On October 24, with the mountaintops dusted in snow and veiled in mist, the Austrian-German Fourteenth Army, including seven German divisions, under the German general Otto von Below, heralded disaster with an intense bombardment with gas and high explosives. The Fourteenth Army, with the Tenth and Fifth Austrian armies on its flanks in support, launched the main effort on the Isonzo front, north of Gorizia. On paper the Italians had superiority—more than forty divisions against the Austrian-German thirty-five—but the Italians were decimated and war weary.

All the hard-won Italian gains in eleven bloody, bruising battles of the Isonzo were wiped out in one thunderbolt attack in the twelfth battle. By the afternoon of the twenty-fourth, Von Below and his Germans were across the Isonzo and the Italian Second Army was routed. What the world knows as Caporetto—then the name of a small Italian village in the vortex of the fight, but now a synonym for disaster—was written in blood.

The Germans used the Von Hutier tactics—utilized in the assault against Riga—surprise, violent short bombardments, infiltration, and by-passing centers of resistance—and their rapid advance trapped many soldiers of the Italian Carnic force in the north.

The Italian Third and Fourth armies, on the flanks of the breakthrough, fell back hurriedly but in good order to avoid entrapment. But thousands of Italians surrendered and cheered their conquerors on, with cries of "Long live Austria," and "On to Rome." The virus of the Bolsheviks had done its work well.

An attempt to stand on the Tagliamento River on November 2 ended in another headlong retreat; by November 7 the broad obstacle of the Piave, seventy miles behind the original Isonzo front, had been reached. Here, not far from the queenly city of Venice, with its ancient glories, the front at last held; the limited German strength, supply difficulties, and the small reserves available for exploitation all combined to slow and halt the Austrian-German effort.

Caporetto was the greatest single disaster of Italian arms in modern history. The Italians suffered more than 300,000 casualties (including 265,000 prisoners). The heart of Italy's rich northern plain was threatened; the enemy captured thousands of guns and tremendous quantities of supplies, and the blow to the national morale appeared crippling. Von Below's stiletto just missed the Italian heart.

Vittorio E. Orlando took the helm as Italy's Premier; Cadorna was relieved by the youthful, fifty-six-year-old General Armando Díaz. By December 12 six French and five British divisions arrived to stiffen the shocked Italians. And out of disaster was foaled the first major step toward unified direction of the Allied war effort. At Rapallo, Italy, in early November, before the Piave Line was finally stabilized, a Supreme War Council was established at Lloyd George's suggestion with both political and military representation. The permanent site of the council was fixed at Versailles, France; the ousted General Cadorna became Italy's representative, and General Ferdinand Foch the French member.

THE MACEDONIAN FRONT

Nineteen-seventeen, on the Macedonian front, was more notable for political intrigue and Allied bickering than for military accomplishments. From the beginning, the Salonikan venture had had neither clear-cut political nor definite military objectives. The Allies had suffered from a guilty conscience—invasion of the soil of a nominal neutral, Greece; from lack of any real unified command; and from the pompous, overbearing personality of the senior general, the French Sarrail, who was titular (but not *de facto*) commander in chief of the Allied armies of the East.

Sarrail launched a general assault on May 9, but the

Serbians, who had captured Monastir in late 1916, were torn and divided, had no confidence in Sarrail, and felt a greater victory had been denied them in 1916 because of lack of support from their allies. The attack died quickly.

In June the Greek problem was at length clarified—if not resolved. Sarrail was authorized to invade Thessaly, where some royalist troops of the Greek Army had remained mobilized. There followed an intricate and devious pattern of both political and military maneuvering, which led on June 12 to the end of the reign of King Constantine. He left the country under Allied pressure, and a pro-Allied Venizelos government, which brought nine divisions into the war, assumed complete control of Greece. On June 29, Greece formally declared war on Germany, Turkey, and Bulgaria.

And December brought more good news: the pettifogging, intriguing Sarrail was relieved by French General Marie Louis Guillaumat.

THE OUTER THEATERS

The dying Turkish empire had one brief respite and two great defeats in 1917.

On the Caucasus front, the Russian pressure ended with the Russian Revolution; from then until war's end, a few feckless Russian soldiers in isolated detachments played inconsequential roles.

But in both Palestine and Mesopotamia the British reinforced success. David Lloyd George, like Winston Churchill, believed in eccentric strategy—attack on an enemy periphery —and in both Palestine and Mesopotamia political objectives superseded military ones.

The Palestine campaign stemmed from the militarily sound concept of defending the Suez Canal by an advance across Sinai to the strategic flanking position near El Arish. This was attained in late 1916 and in the first days of January, 1917. British air reconnaissance, which aided the ground armies greatly in the Palestine theater, placed the retreating Turks in early March in the Gaza-Beersheeba area. Sir Archibald Murray, the British commander in Egypt, was told to undertake a limited holding offensive to keep the Turks busy. He moved to the attack on March 26 in the First Battle of Gaza, with five reinforced divisions opposing about three Turkish divisions. It was a near victory, but bad communications and unwarranted assumptions led to failure, British withdrawal, and 4,000 casualties as against about 2,500 Turkish casualties.

Murray tried again on April 17, but this time against a strengthened Turkish position. Another Turkish division had joined, and Kress von Kressenstein, the wily German, had constructed mutually supporting strong points. The result of a bloody frontal assault was a severe British repulse, 6,400 British casualties, 2,000 Turks. Murray was recalled, and there came to Palestine a redoubtable general, nicknamed "The Bull," who had commanded the Third Army at Arras. General Sir Edmund Allenby knew what he was doing, what he wanted to do, and how. He injected new life into the British forces.

Allenby asked and got reinforcements, and spent the summer in careful preparations. He was given two divisions from Salonika, formed another from bits and pieces in the theater, and by fall seven infantry and three cavalry divisions were ready. The Turks, too, were reinforced, but not strongly. Turkish divisions freed by the Russian collapse had been formed into the so-called Yilderim ("Lightning") Force under the German General von Falkenhayn, and some of these had reached the Gaza front. But the British had at least a two-to-one superiority.

Allenby attacked the Beersheeba-Gaza position on October 31; Beersheeba was captured by dusk after a mounted cavalry charge by an Australian brigade, and Gaza fell on the night of November 6-7. It was victory, but incomplete; the Turks held tenaciously to the key communications junctions which covered their retreat. Both the retreat and the pursuit were governed by an arid land's most precious commodity—water.[24]

The way to Jerusalem was now open. From a defensive

holding operation, the Palestine campaign had grown into a major offensive; Jerusalem had become a glittering political and psychological prize for the war-weary British people. Allenby had brought victory to a people starved for victory; on to Jerusalem!

Supply and communications favored the British. The Turks depended upon a 1,300-mile railroad lifeline, with wood-burning locomotives; the British had organized well their land routes across Sinai, and above all, they possessed the inestimable advantage of command of the sea. The result was inevitable.

On December 8, Allenby launched an assault with four divisions against Turkish positions which stretched from the Mediterranean, north of Jaffa, to angle back southward in the Judean Hills in front of Jerusalem. The Turkish lines bent and broke; on December 9 they retreated from Jerusalem; the Holy City was at last in British hands. In a few days the rains came, and the campaigning season was over.

The Palestine campaign—fought by illiterate Turkish askars, Indian sepoys, rambunctious Australians, Oxford dons, and Prussian junkers, and supplied by man-back, donkeys, camels, mules, horses, railroads, pipelines, and ships —was aided by an Arab revolt, incited, inspired, and organized by British pounds and promises, and by the tortured genius of a young British archaeologist, T. E. Lawrence. During 1917 Lawrence and his Arab bands—mostly camel mounted—harried, cut off, and immobilized Turkish forces along the so-called Hejaz railroad in Arabia. During Allenby's advance into Palestine, Lawrence and his irregulars covered the British right flank, made raids and reconnoitered, and supplied invaluable information about Turkish dispositions. Lawrence was one of that vanishing breed, an intellectual romantic, who was at the same time a man of rugged action, with a natural eye for terrain and an aptitude for soldiering. The Arab revolt and Lawrence, though important, were ancillary to Allenby's success; and Lawrence will live more for a book than a battle—his immortal *Seven Pillars of Wisdom*.

In Mesopotamia, the prize of Baghdad lured British armies

ever northward; Sir Stanley Maude with a quarter of a million men (less than half of them combat troops) far outnumbered the riddled Turks. The battle was as much one of supply as of bullets. River craft in large numbers, laborers, and animals of all kinds formed Maude's lifeline to the sea.

Maude, after stubborn resistance and delay caused by torrential rains, finally cleared the enemy from Kut al Imara, site of a great British defeat, and moved up the Tigris past the Shumran bend and Asiziyeh (March 4), which was developed as an air base for fourteen British planes. Halil Pasha, commanding the weak Turkish Sixth Army—which had one 11,000-man corps in front of Baghdad—attempted to make a stand at Diyala, but he was outmaneuvered and far outnumbered.

The city of the Arabian Nights fell after small-scale fighting on March 11, and a dream of *"Drang nach Osten"*— the Berlin-to-Baghdad railway—was ended.

The British consolidated their hold and Halil Pasha fell back to the north with the tatters of his army. Both sides reinforced during the hot months, and in November Maude moved north again and took Ramadi and Tikrit. It was his last victory. The British general, whose name had become a byword in England, died suddenly of cholera on November 18 "in the house in Baghdad in which (the German commander) Kolmar von der Goltz Pasha had died eighteen months earlier."[25]

In East Africa, 1917 was, strategically, a repetition of 1916. Throughout the year British, Belgian, and other Allied forces tried to corner and destroy the elusive German forces. They were only partially successful. One of Lettow-Vorbeck's principal subordinates, with 13,000 men was finally forced to surrender to the British on November 25. But Lettow-Vorbeck himself, after a heavy battle along the Lukuledi River in the south, escaped with his force across the frontier of Portuguese East Africa. For the first time in more than three years of war, German East Africa was cleared of the enemy.

The year 1917 marked the ultimate transformation of the conflict into a global war. Many Latin American countries followed the United States into the war, and the world patterns of trade, political and economic relations, travel, and scholarship and emotional ties were wrenched and distorted into shapes which would never again assume their prewar forms. Dimly Americans perceived that the golden age had ended. The prospects of a negotiated peace—never very bright—waned with the entry of the United States; for this reason and because America's interposition meant the entry onto the stage of history of a new world power, Major General J. F. C. Fuller has described April 6, 1917, as "the most fateful day in European history since Varus lost his legions. . . ."[26]

Not only politically, but militarily, the war broadened. General Pershing foresaw that Russia's collapse would make 1918 the most dangerous part of the war for the Allies on the Western Front; Germany was certain to make a huge convulsive effort. He asked as early as July that one million American troops be sent to France by May of 1918, rather than the 650,000 the War Department had planned by June, 1918. The tank, successfully demonstrated at Cambrai, made new demands on the factories for guns and armor plate and tracks. The plane had demonstrated for the first time a capability of intervening successfully in the ground battle; in Palestine and Mesopotamia it was helping to turn retreats into routs. Surface raiders—the *Möwe* and the *Wolf*— sank scores of merchantmen and sowed mines off the scented isles of the East and in most of the seven seas. The submarine also showed its terrible reach; U-boats ranged across the oceans, bombarded Ponta Delgada in the Azores, cut cables off the United States coast, and operating from the Adriatic, even supplied arms and weapons to the revolting tribesmen of the desert—the fierce Senusi—who were harrying both the British in Egypt and the Italians in Tripoli. War had never before been so inclusive, so extensive, so ruthless, so destructive.

But for Germany and the Central Powers the victories of 1917 left a somewhat sour taste. The submarine campaign had obviously failed by the year's end. The triumphs on land had never been quite enough; manpower shortages were growing and, worst of all, the unending British blockade had turned the screws of hunger upon the German people. Nineteen-seventeen was for Germany the "Turnip Year."[27]

And the consequences of the Russian Revolution loomed large across the map of the world. The triumph of the Bolsheviks was to change forever the history of a century; its results, fifty years later, are still incalculable. It was a time of revolution, and Petrograd set the pace. The dragon's teeth had been well sown, and watered heavily with blood for three long years; now the seeds were sprouting; scarce a country that could not see the grim harvest. The specter of revolt faced the world—in France, Austria, Germany, Italy, the Senusi and the Arabs and the Irish, nations and races diverse and farflung.

VI

EXHAUSTION AND VICTORY—1918

NINETEEN-EIGHTEEN was the testing time. The great contestants, gasping and bloody, girded for the blows they knew would come. The idealistic schoolmaster, Woodrow Wilson, who stood for "peace without victory," a brotherhood of nations, and the self-determination of peoples, enunciated (January 8) as war aims the famous Fourteen Points (open diplomacy; freedom of the seas; reduction of arms; etc.). But passion tempered idealism; the term "hyphenated American" (German-American) became a phrase of opprobrium; the harsh sedition acts were passed. The people demanded patriotic conformity; enemy nationals, left-wingers, and "Wobblies" incurred the wrath of public feeling and the lash of legislation. Eugene Debs, the pacifist Socialist leader, was sentenced to jail. Nineteen-eighteen was to see the last convulsive German efforts in the West; the final surrender of Russia and Rumania; the Allied build-up; the great offensives in France, Italy, Macedonia, and the Middle East; and the collapse and surrender of Bulgaria, Turkey, Austria-Hungary, and Germany. It was to witness air power—portent for tomorrow—come of age, and the seaways harried to the last by submarine and raider. Nineteen-eighteen was the Wagnerian finale to more than four years of bloodshed unlimited.

The End in the East

The Bolsheviks, hoping for a revolution in Germany, opened 1918 with stalling tactics at Brest-Litovsk, where negotiations for a permanent peace had been started. But all the cards, as Baron Richard von Kuhlmann knew, were held by the Germans. After Trotsky had refused to meet the German terms and had announced his "Neither Peace nor War" policy, Berlin turned the screws. German troops, advancing against little opposition, occupied the Baltic states in February, moved into the Ukraine and Kiev, and even into the Crimea and the Caucasus. Civil war had started in Russia, with the "Whites" opposing the "Reds," and the country was in chaos. Petrograd was threatened by the German advance, and Lenin moved the capital to Moscow. Capitulation was inevitable.

On March 3, the Treaty of Brest-Litovsk was signed by the Russians. It was a harsh peace. Poland, the Baltic provinces, and Finland were severed from Russia. Turkey gained the Kars, Ardahan and Batum areas in the Caucasus, and an independent state of the Ukraine—actually a German puppet, a vast granary for Berlin—was established. Russia lost "26 per cent of its territory, 27 per cent of its cultivated area, 26 per cent of its railroads, 33 per cent of its textile industry, 73 per cent of its iron and steel industry, and 75 per cent of its coal mines."[1] Some, but not all, of this loss was nullified later by Germany's defeat.

Rumania, completely isolated and defeated, signed an even harsher peace in May which made her for the rest of the war virtually a German satrapy.

Organized mayhem was over in the East, and the Germans immediately commenced to transfer divisions to the Western Front.

On November 30, 1917, German divisions in the West numbered 160; at year end, 171; by the end of January, 1918, 175; and on March 21, 194, with a peak strength of 203 divisions still ahead. The bulk of German strength—almost 3,600,000 men—was now concentrated in the West, although more than one million men were still scattered from Turkey and the Balkans through the Ukraine and Poland to Hango, Finland, where a 9,000-man German force landed near Helsinki in April to help Baron Carl von Mannerheim make good Finnish independence against Red opposition.[2]

Russia was out of the war, but war's fevers still raged in Russia. Anti-Bolshevik armies struggled against the Reds on many detached fronts—in the Ukraine, the Caucasus, Siberia, and elsewhere. One large group of about 40,000 men—the Czechoslovak Legion, which had been formed of deserters and prisoners from the Austro-Hungarian armies—had participated in the final Kerensky offensive. It opposed the Brest-Litovsk peace and the Bolshevist government, was determined to fight with the Allies in the West, and in an epic anabasis commenced to make its way across the heart of Russia toward Vladivostok. This group soon seized the Trans-Siberian railroad and sparked an anti-Bolshevist rising in Siberia. Its troops approached Ekaterinburg in the Urals, where the Czar and his family had been imprisoned by the Bolsheviks on July 16. A frightened local soviet, fearful that the Czar would be restored, ordered and supervised the execution of Nicholas II, last of the Romanov dynasty, his wife and children, and all their now pitifully small entourage. Death in a mean cellar was the end of a royal road.

But the war of brother against brother, people against people, class against class had just started; Kolchak, Denikin, and other White Russian leaders opposed Budënny, Stalin, and other Bolshevists in no-quarter ruthless fighting.

A mixed variety of motives led to Allied involvement in the Russian civil wars. Hope that some Russian war effort against Germany might be encouraged, fear that large quantities of ammunition and supplies might be seized by the Bolsheviks, a desire to aid the Czech Legion, fear of Bolshevism, and for some—notably the Japanese—political aspirations, combined to rationalize Allied intervention in North Russia and in Siberia. Militarily, such expeditions represented a dispersion of effort; politically, there was no clear-cut objective. Nevertheless, early in the spring of 1918 small British detach-

ments moved into Murmansk and Archangel and were subsequently reinforced by French, Serbian, Polish, White Russian, and American forces. Ultimately almost 5,000 Americans
—the 339th Infantry Regiment reinforced—took part in the
North Russian occupation and endured the rigors of a
Russian winter and bitter fighting against the Bolsheviks,
before they were finally withdrawn in August, 1919. Allied
forces also moved into Vladivostok and Siberia. Major
General William S. Graves, with 10,000 Americans (27th
and 31st Infantry Regiments reinforced) under Japanese
supreme command, safeguarded rail lines and supply dumps
from Vladivostok to Lake Baikal, and checkmated Japanese
expansionist ambitions. The American force was withdrawn
by April, 1920.[3]

THE WAR AT SEA

By January, 1918, the German unrestricted submarine
campaign had been definitely checked, though the menace
never ended. More than 306,000 tons of Allied and neutral
shipping were sunk by submarines in January; the sinkings
reached their 1918 peak in March when 342,000 tons were
destroyed. But never again during the war did the monthly
losses reach 300,000 tons and by the second quarter of 1918
world shipyards were more than replacing the tonnage that
was sunk.

The convoy system was the principal defense. Not a single
American troop transport was lost on its way to France. But
all kinds of weapons, techniques, and methods were employed
to cripple the submarine. The German Navy had 134 submarines in commission in January, 1918; it lost 73 and completed 85 during the year.

The development and refinement of radio direction finding
helped the Allies to locate German submarines at sea, when
surfaced. Underwater sound instruments—listening "ears"
or hydrophones—were helpful at short distances. Some three
thousand Allied destroyers, sub-chasers, and small craft were
equipped with sound gear. Mines, other submarines, depth

charges, gunfire, decoy ships, nets, and—at the last—bombs dropped by planes accounted for most of the 178 German submarines sunk during the war.

The Dover barrage of nets and mines which stretched across the Strait was strengthened considerably by Admiral Sir Roger Keyes, and took a heavy toll of German U-boats early in the year. An attempt by Admiral Scheer to break the barrage by destroyers on February 15 sank eight British small craft, guarding the nets. Another raid was made in March, but the barrage remained and became more and more effective, though never completely so.

A companion barrage—but tremendous in size and scope —to block the northern egress from the North Sea between the Orkneys and the coast of Norway was incompletely laid between May and November. A new type of U.S.-invented mine, with a long antenna, was used, and during 1918 U.S. naval forces laid 56,571 mines, the British 13,546, in the largest project of its kind ever attempted—the North Sea mine barrage. It added to the hazards of U-boat sorties, and probably accounted for several submarines, but again it did not completely "seal the varmints" in their nests.

Admiral Keyes commanded still another attempt to bottle up two of the important U-boat bases at Zeebrugge and Ostend—a blockship operation in the best Nelsonian tradition. Five old cruisers, filled with concrete, escorted by the old cruiser *Vindictive* and other ships (about seventy in all), made the attempt on the night of April 22-23. *Vindictive*, with a storming party aboard, was put alongside the mole at Zeebrugge, encouraged by a signal from Keyes: "St. George for England."[4]

In the bloody fracas the blockships were sunk successfully in the Channel at Zeebrugge, but the Ostend attempt was a failure. British losses were 189 killed, 383 wounded, 16 missing, plus one destroyer and two motor launches. The Germans lost one destroyer. A later attempt—May 9-10—to seal Ostend was partially successful.

In the Mediterranean, the German battle cruiser *Goeben* and light cruiser *Breslau* which had been, nominally, part of the Turkish fleet since 1914, attempted to break out of the Dardanelles on January 20, 1918, apparently to join the Austrian fleet in the Adriatic. The attempt, which won initial success, was abortive. Two British monitors at Imbros were surprised and sunk with a loss of 133 killed, but the *Breslau* struck a mine shortly afterward and sank after a series of explosions. The *Goeben* also struck a mine, turned back, was beached in the Dardanelles and attacked repeatedly by British planes and submarines. She survived to reach Constantinople for repairs.

Allied efforts to seal the Adriatic were strengthened and improved. A patrolled barrage of mines and nets from Otranto to Corfu, guarded by a variety of small craft, including thirty-six U.S. wooden 110-foot sub-chasers of the "splinter fleet," made submarine passage hazardous. Admiral Miklós Horthy, Austrian naval commander, attempted to break the barrage in June by a sortie from the bases at Pola and Cattaro by destroyers, cruisers, and battleships. Commander Luigi Rizzo of the Italian Navy, who in December, 1917, had sunk the Austrian coast defense ship *Wien* at anchor at Trieste, repeated his feat in the open sea in the early dark hours of June 10. His little coastal motor boat torpedoed and sank the Austrian dreadnought *Szent Istvan* in the upper Adriatic; the barrage at the Strait of Otranto continued to function.

Later in the year, on the eve of Armistice (October 31–November 1), the Italians—who were the original "frogmen" and chalked up a long series of daring small-craft actions—penetrated Pola harbor, despite booms and shore defenses, on man-handled "torpedoes," and, with limpet mines, sank the Austrian battleship *Viribus Unitis* and an auxiliary cruiser. That very night the Austrian crews had mutinied; the ships were in the hands of Yugoslav sailors.[5]

Throughout 1918, the operations of the U.S. Navy increased in variety, scope, and strength. Of the more than 2,000,000 American troops that were transported to France—1,500,000 of them in the last six months of the war—about 49 to 50 percent were transported in British ships, 45 percent in American. "On the whole, the safeguarding of American soldiers on the ocean was an achievement of the American Navy," Admiral Sims declared. About 82 percent of the escort job was done by U.S. naval vessels.[6]

The United States Navy also operated three dirigibles, fifty kite balloons, and four hundred planes for reconnaissance, patrol, and antisubmarine warfare in the United States, France, the British Isles, and the Mediterranean. The U.S. Naval Northern Bombing Group (with 112 planes) attacked German submarine bases in Zeebrugge and Ostend. The navy also designed, tested, built, and operated in France five railway-mounted 14-inch guns—the largest pieces of ordnance available to the Allied armies. From August until the Armistice these guns fired 782 shells at ranges of eighteen to twenty-three miles.[7]

The German High Seas Fleet, save for one or two abortive sorties, was quiescent in 1918—gripped already with the dry rot of defeat. Disaffections in the summer were quieted, but in the dying days of the Kaiser's Germany, on October 28, 1918, as the German admirals prepared to put to sea for a final battle of immolation, mutiny spread from *Thüringen* to *Helgoland* and throughout the fleet—and then to the land. "On Nov. 9, William II lamented that he had 'no longer a Navy' ";[8] he might have added, or a country either.

THE WAR IN THE AIR

In 1918, the airplane came of age. In all phases of warfare the plane—in 1914 a puling infant of Mars—participated with lusty effectiveness. Combat aircraft with speeds of 160 miles an hour and ceilings of more than 20,000 feet were in operation. In Britain, the Royal Flying Corps became the Royal Air Force on April 1, 1918, and in May the U.S. Army Air Service, divorced from the Signal Corps, was established. A so-called "Independent Air Force" was organized by the British near Nancy during the summer. It dropped more than five hundred tons of bombs on German industrial and communications targets, using De Havilland day bombers and the big Handley-Page night bombers, which had an eight-hour endurance and could carry more than 1,700 pounds of bombs. The German raids on London, on the other hand, declined in 1918; the last was in May when seven raiders were shot down. As late as September, however, German Gothas were attacking Paris.

On July 19, 1918, the British also made history by flying seven Sopwith Camel planes off the deck of the aircraft carrier *Furious* (hastily converted from an 18-inch-gunned battle-cruiser hull) to bomb successfully German Zeppelin bases at Tondern.[9]

All these beginnings of what was later to be known as "strategic bombing"—in which both sides and all the principal combatants participated—had some depressant effect upon morale, increased industrial absenteeism and reduced output, sent thousands to the shelters of the London subways at night, and caused the diversion of considerable effort to the defense, but over-all had only a small ancillary effect upon the war.

Air power's intervention in the ground battle was, however, more effective and more diverse. The 1918 ground battles were everywhere accompanied or preceded by battles in the skies; sometimes hundreds of airplanes were twisting and turning in dogfights. Bombing behind the lines, strafing of troops and artillery positions, reconnaissance, artillery spotting, and photography were all part of the plane's role. At the Second Battle of the Marne and at the Piave in Italy the air bombardment of bridges was a major factor in stalling the German and Austrian offensives. In Palestine, the plane showed at Megiddo how defeat could be turned into rout.

The size of the air forces, tiny when war started, became tremendous. Toward the end of the war, the British were operating all over the world about 2,600 aircraft; the French about 3,857; the Germans 2,800; the Italians more than 800; the U.S. Army Air Service about 740 (in squadrons behind the front, plus about 400 U.S. Naval planes); the Austrians 600; and the Belgians about 150.

The tiny Lafayette Escadrille, composed of American volunteer fliers who served with the French a year before the United States entered the war, grew to U.S. air services of more than a quarter of a million men. These fliers trained largely in U.S.-built trainers—the famous "Jenny," (Curtiss JN4's). But less then one-fifth (1,200 out of 6,300) of the planes delivered to the American Expeditionary Force were actually built in the United States, and all of them—the British De Havilland 4 (the notorious "flaming coffins"), the British Handley-Page, the Italian Caproni, the British Bristol, and the French Spad, Nieuport, and Breguet—were of foreign design. In observation balloons the United States chalked up a better record; the nation produced 642 and actually floated in France 369.

These new fliers produced their own leaders, their own heroes, their own brand of hard-shelled romanticism, their own argot, and their own methods and tactics. Major General Sir Hugh Trenchard in England was the father of Britain's Royal Air Force and probably the greatest high-ranking air leader of the war. Brigadier General William ("Billy") Mitchell, U.S.A., was a dynamic, enthusiastic believer in air power, well ahead of his time in ideas and vision. Such American fliers as Raoul Lufbery, Eddie Rickenbacker, Frank Luke, and many others quickly became air aces. Theirs was short life expectancy—most of them flew without parachutes —but never dull moments. Of 2,698 planes sent to the U.S. zones for the use of American pilots, only some 1,100 were still flying at the Armistice.

The American Army Air Service pilots claimed more than 750 German planes destroyed against losses of less than half that number. But, like the U.S. ground forces, they did not shoulder the main burden of the air war; the British and the French exceeded the U.S. in numbers, experience, planes.

The air war in 1918 reached crescendo in combat as well as maturity in technology and capability. The Germans in the first part of the year matched their offensive ground capabilities with superior pursuit planes—Albatross single seaters, Fokker triplanes and biplanes, and the Pfalz.

But beginning in July and continuing throughout the great Allied offensives for the rest of the year the Germans were overwhelmed by numbers as the greatest air concentrations of the war—American, British, French, Italian—reconnoitered, photographed, strafed, and bombed. More than eight thousand Allied combat planes were flying over all the battlefronts—perhaps 5,200 of them in France.[10]

In the air, as on the ground, the multifront war—the war of attrition—was a conflict the Germans could not win.

THE MACEDONIAN FRONT

General Guillaumat, energetic and able, shook the Macedonian front out of the doldrums of politics and feuds and prepared plans for a grand offensive. Before he could execute them he was recalled to Paris in July, 1918, to become military governor and to prepare the city for defense in the Second Battle of the Marne. Another fine soldier, Franchet d'Esperey, succeeded him, and after cajoling the politicians in Allied capitals, he was finally allowed to strike on September 15, as the sun of the Central Powers was setting.

He had some 550,000 men, a mixed batch of many Allies, opposed to about 430,000 Bulgars with a thin stiffening of Germans. The Germans commanded the Eleventh Army but the bulk of their strength had been drained away for the Western Front. The Bulgars had precipitous terrain to aid them. But d'Esperey used manpower, tractors, and tackle to haul guns to seven-thousand-foot mountaintops; the Allies attacked with fury—the Serbs joyously—and soon the Bulgars, rotten with disease, low in morale, collapsed.

In two days a twenty-five-mile penetration had been made; on the nineteenth the Serbs were across the Vardar; a general retreat which turned quickly into a rout was started and the enemy front was split in two. Bulgarian representatives signed an armistice—the terms dictated by d'Esperey—on the last day of September, and the first of the Central Powers had been knocked out of the war. Serbian troops moved against weak German opposition back into their country; the Italians advanced up the Adriatic coast to Scutari in Montenegro, and d'Esperey led a French force across Bulgaria—by the terms of the armistice, the Allies were permitted to use Bulgarian railroads and roads—and established a bridgehead across the Danube into Rumania on November 10. His help came a year too late for the Rumanians but he was in time to arrange an armistice in Belgrade with a revolutionary Hungarian government.[11]

The British troops turned east toward the frontiers of Turkey, a fact which was not lost on the desperate Turkish government. The Bulgarian collapse set the stage; Turkey was next. Thus Macedonia, born in confusion, reared in desperation, ended in glory. But it had been, until the end, a costly sideshow for the Allies; about half the Bulgarian Army, with German stiffening, had held down a quarter of a million to half a million men.[12]

THE TURKISH FRONTS

The hapless Turks, riddled by defeats, drained by desertions, and short of supplies, offered no threat in Mesopotamia, little in Palestine.

In Mesopotamia, political and economic considerations led first to the detachment of British troops to North Persia and the Caucasus, then to a British advance along the Tigris in late October. A Turkish force of some seven thousand men surrendered at Sharqat on October 30. Mosul, the oil center, the objective of the British thrust, was occupied by the British on November 14. Mesopotamia was another theater which ate up Allied strength with no commensurate military return (but major postwar political and economic prizes). Almost nine hundred thousand men of many races (chiefly Indian, but also natives of Mauritius, Chinese, Assyrian cavalry, and Arabs) were posted first and last to Mesopotamia throughout the war, and the British empire suffered nearly 92,500 wounded, missing, and prisoners and about 27,600 killed in action or dead of wounds or disease.

In Palestine, 1918 was quiescent until the fall. Reorganiza-

tion, torrential rains, and then the demands of the Western
Front for troops—Allenby shipped about 60,000 men to
France—prevented any large-scale active British operations.
By October, Allenby, reinforced with two divisions from
Mesopotamia, more Indian troops, and a few French (with
an eye on Syria), was ready and Aleppo—key junction point
on the railroad from Constantinople to Baghdad—was the
immediate objective; the capitulation of Turkey the ultimate one.

On September 19, Allenby launched his long-prepared
thunderbolt against the tattered battalions of Liman von
Sanders, who had relieved Falkenhayn. Allenby had better
than a two-to-one numerical superiority, plus almost complete mastery of the skies, the latter a factor that was becoming more and more important in war. The Turks, with
a handful of Germans, were holding a sixty-five-mile front
from the sea to the Jordan Valley. The British launched a
five-division attack against the Turkish-German front along
the coastal plain north of Jaffa; in about three hours they
had made a complete breakthrough and cavalry was exploit-
ing the gap. The Holy Land echoed to the thunder of the
guns, but the Turks were in full retreat.

In two days British cavalry had seized the defiles and road
and rail exits from the Judean Hills; British infantry had
forced the Jordan, and the famed Battle of Megiddo ended
in rout and disaster—one of the most complete defeats of
the war. Remnants of the fleeing Turkish Seventh and Eighth
armies were slaughtered in the narrow valleys by the Royal
Air Force, and the cavalry rounded up thousands of dejected
askars. To the east of the Jordan the Turkish Fourth Army,
harried by T. E. Lawrence's Arab Northern Army and British
horsemen, staggered back to Damascus to surrender, along
with the sun-baked Biblical city on September 30. In the
ruck of defeat, perhaps the greatest rout of the war, the
German contingents—small in number but large in discipline—earned the respect of their foes. Around them flowed
the torrents of disaster: the shapeless units, the faceless men,
the flotsam and jetsam of a great retreat. The Germans, about
two regiments strong, kept their cohesion and their fighting

spirit; they maneuvered as if on parade, halted to fire, moved again to the rear.

It was "glorious," as T. E. Lawrence noted, but it was of no avail. Using sea support for supply and speed, and land transport from the Levant ports, Allenby pushed on to the north against weak opposition. Beirut was opened as a British supply port on October 10; Tripoli on the fourteenth, Aleppo was captured on the twenty-eighth, and the British counted their spoils—75,000 prisoners, more than three hundred guns, booty of all kinds, thousands of enemy casualties, at a cost of 5,666 killed, wounded, and missing. It was over, save for the recriminations and the regrets.

Turkey had had enough. British and Turkish representatives signed an armistice late on October 30 aboard the British battleship *Agamemnon* (aptly named) in Mudros Bay, and on November 12 an Allied fleet, the British in the van, steamed proudly past Gallipoli and through the narrow Straits, past the queen of cities into the Black Sea. Constantinople, where the tides of East and West had warred for so many centuries, had fallen, but the memories of the great repulse of 1915 lingered on.

Turkey, second of the Central Powers, was out of the war, maimed by casualties and waning hope. At Armistice she had a scant half million men in the field, only a fifth of them combat effectives; the rest of her once great host had died in battle, by disease, or had deserted.[13]

But it had been for Britain an expensive campaign in a theater which had more political than military importance. And before the war was over the aftermath of bitterness began. Broken promises to the Arabs and the Balfour Declaration of November, 1917, which described Palestine as a Jewish "national home," boded trouble for the future. Triumph often breeds its own defeats.

THE ITALIAN FRONT

The disaster of Caporetto in the fall of 1917—a terrible depressant to Italian and Allied hopes at the time—ultimately led to a renaissance of Rome's war effort. Under the leadership of Orlando and Díaz Italian determination and will-to-fight were strengthened, the ravages of defeat repaired, and war production increased.

It was time, for on June 13, the Austrians—urged on by the Germans—launched a two-pronged offensive by Conrad's Tenth and Eleventh armies from the Trentino, and by Boroevic von Bojna's Army Group along the Piave. The objectives were the important rail junctions of Verona, Vicenza, and Padua. The offensive was doomed before it started. Forces were about equal—some sixty Austrian divisions, many below strength, against fifty Italian and six Allied divisions. The Austrians had a few more guns, the Allies a few more planes. But the Italians had the advantage of interior position and good communications; the Austrians, with a large part of their front in the mountains, could not readily shift reserves. Accordingly they compromised; instead of making one of the pincers overwhelmingly strong they divided the reserves between Conrad and Boroevic, so that neither had sufficient strength. Conrad made a few gains in the mountains, but quickly lost them to counterattack, and for a time there was a dangerous Austrian bridgehead on a wide front across the Piave about five miles deep. But the Italians had reserves and mobility; counterattack reduced the bridgeheads by July 6, and the last-gasp offensive of the Austrian empire was a failure.

Retribution overtook Conrad; this "remarkable soldier," as Cyril Falls calls him, was dismissed—ignominious end to years of power and glory.

Díaz carefully prepared an offensive against the hapless Austrians for the remainder of the summer and fall: Allied victories in France finally prodded him into action. He was slow in starting; late October rains delayed the offensive until October 24, anniversary of Caporetto. But both time and fortune were on his side. On paper the forces were approximately equal, though the Italians by now had built up a marked superiority in artillery. But Díaz had as spearhead forces the Tenth Army, commanded by a British general, Lord Cavan, with two British divisions (a third British division served in the mountains); two French divisions; and a U.S. regiment, the 32nd of the 83rd Division, sent to Italy in July for morale and political purposes, also added temper to the Italian mass. The Austrians, on the other hand, were sick, war weary, under strength, and divided; facing them on the Italian side was a Czechoslovak division made up of deserters and willing prisoners once in the army of the empire. At home, that empire was breaking up, the people were hungry and discouraged; too late and too little, the Emperor Carl had made political concessions to his vast conglomerate of peoples, but the "federal state" he proclaimed was stillborn.

Nevertheless, high swift water, determined resistance at a few points, and lack of good coordination—an Italian weakness—made the first attempts to cross the Piave touch and go. An attack in the mountains was beaten off, but finally, spearheaded by British and French troops, bridgeheads were established. (The British waded waist deep in the Piave's cold torrents and some were swept from their feet to drown.) Disaster, disintegration, and dissolution followed swiftly. Hungarian troops refused to fight; the town of Vittorio Veneto, which gave the battle its name, was captured on October 30; the Austrian front was broken; retreat turned into rout; and as in Palestine, horsed cavalry came in the fading days of the war to brief glory, harrying the stragglers and rounding up huge hordes of prisoners on the ground, while Allied planes chivvied and slaughtered from the air. Trent in the mountains was captured; the entire front, in gaps and tatters, fell back beyond the Isonzo and into the Carnic Alps. By November 4—date of a hastily arranged armistice—Trieste had been taken by an Italian naval expedition, half a million prisoners had been rounded up, and the last of Germany's allies—what was left of the ancient suzerainty of the late Emperor Franz Josef—had capitulated.

THE WESTERN FRONT

The German strategy for 1918 was simple: to concentrate maximum effort on the Western Front and to win the war or at least force a favorable peace before American reinforcements could tip the scales.

Haig anticipated the German blows, as did Pétain. Both knew the Allies were in no condition in the first half of 1918 to mount an offensive. In fact, 1919 was envisaged as the year of decision.

Ludendorff's plans contemplated a gigantic breakthrough on the Somme, to be followed, if necessary, by a series of sledgehammer offensives to extend the battle and to wear down and disintegrate the war-weary French and British.

As spring came to the long swathe of shell-scarred ground that stretched across France, the German plans seemed cogent. There were only six complete American divisions in France (with supply troops, less than 300,000 men) by March, 1918, and on the right flank of the British armies along the Somme, 71 German divisions, with 2,500 large-calibre guns, faced 26 British with less than one thousand pieces of heavy artillery.[14]

The German offensive in the Second Battle of the Somme was directed against the southern flank of the British front, held in March, 1918, by Byng's Third Army, and Hubert Gough's Fifth Army. Three German armies—Von Below's Seventeenth, fresh from Caporetto, the Second; and Von Hutier's Eighteenth from the Eastern Front—spearheaded the assault. The Germans had carefully trained their divisions in the Von Hutier tactics which had been so successful at Riga and Caporetto. The troops had been taught to forget all they had so painfully learned about trench warfare and to adapt themselves to mobility. Short intensive artillery preparations, a creeping barrage, bypassing of strong points, massive infiltration, and continued forward movement were the earmarks. Ludendorff hoped to crash through the British front, turn north toward the sea, and roll up the British armies.

And he nearly did. Both the British and the French knew the assault was coming, and approximately where, but they underestimated its power.

The British were limited, too, by inadequate reserves. Lloyd George mistrusted Haig's propensity for bloody offensives, and to control Haig's aggressiveness he insisted upon retaining in England large forces of troops. With but few replacements available Haig had to skeletonize his divisions.

On a forty-four-mile front from La Bassée to La Fère the attack opened before dawn on March 21. The British batteries were drenched with gas and silenced, high explosives harried the trenches, and under cover of a fog, which handicapped the attack even more than the defense, the massive German assault made quick progress.

The Germans made fourteen miles in four days—the longest advance on the Western Front since 1914. By March 24 the Germans thought the battle was won; they were in Peronne; the devastated area they had evacuated the year before was again in their hands. The vital rail junction of Amiens was threatened, and the French and British were scraping up divisions from other sections of the front and hurrying them frantically toward the Somme. At this critical junction a unique German gun and Allied cross purposes seemed to provide the final building blocks for disaster.

A sudden explosion in Paris killed a number of people. It was followed by others. Air bombardment was at first blamed, but it was soon learned that the Germans were shelling the city with an extraordinary long-range gun. From emplacements seventy to eighty miles away, the gun lobbed 8-inch shells into the French capital, an example of Teutonic ingenuity which did not help French morale.

Even more important were the misunderstandings and differing views of Haig and Pétain. Pétain told Haig he had ordered the French reinforcing divisions which were on their way to the British right flank to fall back to the southwest to cover Paris if the Germans pressed their attack against Amiens. Pétain believed, though he did not say so, that the British were preparing to fall back to the north to cover the Channel ports. Such diverging retirements would mean the separation of the French and British armies, and possibly their destruction in detail.

This contretemps led first (March 26) to the appointment of General (later Marshal) Ferdinand Foch as coordinator of the British-French forces on the Western Front, then (April 3) to his appointment as commander in chief of all Allied armies in France. It was a title more restricted than it sounds, and often Foch had to accomplish by tact what he could not do by command, but at long last, out of dire emergency, was born a unified command. This alone was worth defeat.

A stalwart British stand on March 28 turned back the Germans and the Second Battle of the Somme died out by April 5, with Amiens still in Allied hands, and the break-through plugged with most of the available reserves. Lloyd George and General Sir Henry Wilson, chief of the Imperial General Staff, demanded a victim. Despite Haig's protests, General Sir Hubert Gough, Fifth Army commander, was replaced by General Sir Henry Rawlinson. It had been a near thing; the British had lost about 160,000 men, including 90,000 prisoners, and their morale and that of their French allies, who suffered more than 70,000 casualties, had had a bad knock. The Germans had captured tremendous booty; they had re-established much of the old Noyon salient and were within seven miles of Amiens. But they had also forced what Allied deliberations had not been able to effect in four long years: an Allied unified command.

The Germans struck their second sledgehammer blow at the Battle of Lys on a twelve-mile front just south of Ypres from April 9-30. The key rail junction of Hazebrouck, and then, if possible, the Channel coast, were the objectives. Most of the sixty British divisions in France had been en-gaged at one time or another in the Somme battle; many of them had been cut to pieces and were absorbing replace-ments when the blow fell. A second-rate Portuguese division was squarely in its path; it departed precipitously and left a gaping hole. A battered British division, still gasping from the Somme, also gave way, and by April 12, Haig had com-mitted his last reserves, and the German ten-mile advance (seventeen miles at its extreme penetration) had moved so close to Hazebrouck there was little room for maneuver. Haig issued his famous "backs to the wall" order:

There is no other course open to us but to fight it out. Every position must be held to the last man. . . . With our backs to the wall and believing in the justice of our cause each one must fight on to the end.

British planes strafed and bombed the attacking Germans furiously, but the Germans quickly captured most of Messines Ridge, and the British gave up that bloody ground, so long fought for, in the Ypres salient. The fighting was extended to the quiet Belgian front, but the Germans were heavily repulsed in the coastal lowlands, and with seven French reserve divisions moving into the line—the first fruit of the Foch unified direction—it was all over by the end of April.

But the British had been bled white; their divisions were in tatters, gasping and spent; reinforcements and replacements were funneled to France from England, Italy, Palestine, and Macedonia.

The Allies had lost at least 350,000 casualties in six weeks of fighting; the Germans not many less. Ludendorff determined to pin down the French and draw their reserves away from Flanders. The third great German blow—the Third Battle of the Aisne—struck the French (plus some British divisions resting in a "quiet" sector) on May 27 on a twenty-five-mile front with forty-two divisions, nineteen in the initial assault. The Chemin des Dames, so dearly bought, was wrenched from the French, and the Germans were across the Aisne in a deep ten-mile penetration on the first day; by June 2-3, they had reached the Marne at Château-Thierry, fifty-six miles from Paris. A salient about thirty-two miles deep at its maximum with a base of fifty miles had been hammered into the French lines.

In the emergency General Pershing assigned the 2nd and 3rd U.S. divisions to the French. A machine-gun battalion of the 3rd Division, under command of the French Sixth Army, assisted the French in repulsing German attempts to cross the Marne at Château-Thierry. Two brigades helped the French reduce German bridgeheads at Jaulgonne. The 3rd had never before been under fire, but it earned high French commendation. The 2nd Division, attacking throughout June and early July on the western flank of the salient's apex, took Vaux and Bouresches, and Belleau Wood in hard-fought, bloody actions. The Marine brigade, serving with the 2nd—its men known as "Leathernecks" or "Devil Dogs" —won its immortality in nineteen days of searing fighting. But the casualties were terrible: 40 percent for many of the combat units. In the meantime, on May 28 in the first test of American combat effectiveness, the 1st U.S. Division took and held, in a neatly planned and executed operation, the strongly held village of Cantigny at the apex of the great Amiens salient.

American arms had been bloodied; the test of battle had found them inexperienced, but brave and apt pupils. More important, these first appearances of American combat troops in "hot" sectors of the front (small numbers of medical, engineer, and air units had supported the British in the Somme and Lys battles) had brought renewed hope to the tired Allies. The Americans were big men; they marched proud and tall; and there were millions more behind them.

And it was well there were. Ever since the first great German drive in 1918, the Supreme War Council had sent emergency pleas for help to Washington. Infantry and machine-gun units had the highest priority; the French and British wanted to integrate them into their chewed-up divisions. Pershing understood the dire need, but throughout the war he insisted upon the ultimate objective of forming an American army to fight as an army under its own command. Troop transport was speeded; and in early June, Lloyd George, Clemenceau, and Orlando asked for one hundred American divisions, some four million men, and pointed out that only the United States could redress the adverse balance of forces on the Western Front, where some 162 Allied divisions faced more than 200 German divisions (on June 1, Allied combat strength, as measured by riflemen totaled about 1,450,000 men; German, 1,640,000).[15]

On June 9, in an attempt to expand the base of the Marne salient and to link it with the great Amiens bulge, the Germans launched their fourth great offensive, with thirteen divisions—their objective the Montdidier-Compiègne-Soissons Railway. The hard-worked German General von Hutier, with the Eighteenth Army, again proved that his tactics of mobile infiltration were sound. He made a six-mile gain—tremendous by the standards of 1915-1917, but not enough in these last convulsive bids for victory.

The Germans were almost through; at home war weariness and food shortages and subversion were undermining morale; at the front, the tall strange Western men—the "Yankees"—were coming fresh and cocky in ever greater numbers.

The fifth and final German drive—a three-day offensive launched on July 15—is now known to history as the Second Battle of the Marne or the Champagne-Marne. It was intended as a gigantic diversion to draw French forces away from the British front where the ultimate blow was to be struck. The high tide of the German advance lapped at much the same ground covered by the first great drive of 1914, but it was far less dangerous.

"Ils ne passeront pas!" was again the rallying cry, and now, unlike 1914, there were nine American and two Italian divisions, plus twenty-three French divisions to stem the tide (and several British divisions in reserve, transferred from the British front). The Germans tried with maximum strength—fifty-two divisions—in assaults east and west of Rheims, to extend the base of the Marne salient and to cross the Marne. One-armed, redoubtable General Henri Gouraud, commanding the French Fourth Army, had prepared elastic defenses in depth east of Rheims and the Germans got nowhere. To the west of Rheims the Germans crossed the Marne on a wide front, and established bridgeheads four miles deep while Clemenceau fumed. But Foch was not worried; already the cool competent chess player had prepared his riposte, and a hail of bombs and artillery fire virtually interdicted the German supply routes across the Marne bridges. By the eighteenth the last great German drive had failed and the soldiers in the coal-scuttle helmets were moving north of the river again. Once again the river Marne, held by men who would not let them pass, had saved France.

It was the final turning point. Pétain and Foch and Pershing had all foreseen that the first six months of 1918 would be the crucial days; by July, U.S. strength would be adequate to permit Allied offensives.

By mid-July there were twenty-nine U.S. divisions in France or on their way, almost one million men. Some 85,000 Americans—three divisions—had been in action in the Second Battle of the Marne; a U.S. corps (the I Corps under General Hunter Liggett) was holding a section of the front, and U.S. units of various size from battalions to divisions were scattered along much of the front. There were nine U.S. divisions in France in April; eighteen at the end of May; twenty-five at the end of June; twenty-nine at the end of July; thirty-five at the end of August; thirty-nine at the end of September; forty-two at the end of October. The "bridge of ships" across the Atlantic was transporting 250,000 to 300,000 troops a month.[16] In mid-June German rifle strength on the Western Front, decimated by casualties, had fallen below Allied rifle strength; from then on it was all downhill for the armies of the Kaiser.

Ludendorff had cast the dice; once again the gray-clad hosts had moved almost within sight of the spires of Paris. The Germans had captured about 225,000 prisoners in their 1918 offensives, inflicted a total of almost one million casualties; yet their triumphs were a "victory without a morrow." It was Foch's turn.

From July 18, when Foch mounted his first riposte, throughout the rest of 1918, the Allies conducted an almost continuous offensive on the Western Front. The first hammer blows were directed at the great salients the Germans had driven into the Allied lines: the Aisne-Marne; the Amiens-Somme-Noyon; the Lys-Ypres; and St.-Mihiel. After the reduction of the salients, the final drives were aimed at breakthrough and triumph, which, it was felt, might not occur until 1919.

Peppery General Mangin led the French Tenth Army in a hard drive against the west flank of the Aisne-Marne salient on July 18. The 1st and 2nd American divisions under his command drove deep into the enemy flank, south of Soissons, and soon there was action around the entire bulge as converging attacks reduced the salient. The battle dragged on until August 6, with hard fighting and limited gains, but with the pocket slowly shrinking. Eight U.S. divisions (270,-000 men) and a number of British divisions participated, but the bulk of the troops were French. The battle ended with two U.S. corps in line, Soissons recaptured, and the Vesle reached. The successful counteroffensive spoiled Ludendorff's plans for another blow at the British and convinced some in Berlin that "all was lost."[17] The Aisne-Marne battle is regarded by some historians as a continuation of the Second Battle of the Marne.

Foch was anxious to free the French lateral railroads, with important junctions at Amiens and Hazebrouck, from German threat. The Amiens-Somme-Noyon salient was next on the Allied list. Henry Rawlinson's British Fourth Army, with the French First and Third, attacked near the apex of the salient on August 8. Rawlinson with eleven divisions in assault (four, including one U.S. division, in reserve), 450 tanks, heavy artillery support, and 374 planes achieved surprise, and by the fifteenth Montdidier was recaptured, the bulge flattened out, and the threat to Amiens relieved. The Canadian Corps led the twelve-mile advance, and the British and French rounded up about 30,000 prisoners and inflicted, for one of the few times in the West, considerably more casualties (perhaps 50,000 to 60,000) than they suffered.

Ludendorff was later to call August 8 "the black day of the German Army." For the first time German soldiers straggled in large numbers; reserves moving to the front were greeted with shouts of derision by disorderly units moving to the rear. The cement of discipline—the Germans' strongest asset—was weakening. At a conference at Spa, the German GHQ, at which the Kaiser presided, it was decided on August 14 that a favorable opportunity must be found to seek peace.

Ludendorff hailed "another black day" on August 20, as the battle was extended by Haig and Foch to both flanks from Arras to Soissons. The British First and Third armies

to the north and the French Tenth Army near Soissons drove
hard in converging assaults between August 19 and 21. The
few yards so bitterly won in 1917 were now becoming miles.
Mangin reached the Oise, the British made major gains
around Arras. Ludendorff ordered about a ten-mile withdrawal on a fifty-five-mile front. The Somme was crossed;
Péronne was won by the Australians. On into September,
the Allies continued the rataplan of blows against the weakening German front.

It was too much. The Germans abandoned the Lys-Ypres
salient, and pulled back out of the Somme-Noyon bulge,
back again across the devastated, tortured earth to the Hindenburg Line. Back where they had started from in the hope-
ful spring months. The retirement was stubborn and
orderly; supplies were evacuated, scorched earth left behind,
mines and roads and bridges and villages destroyed, while the
heavy field fortifications of the Hindenburg Line, long prepared, were strengthened and amplified. On September 25,
the retirement was finished; the Allies were facing the key
German defensive system.

In the meantime, as the Somme-Noyon bulge and Lys-
Ypres salient were being eliminated, the American Army,
operating for the first time as an army, reduced the St.-
Mihiel salient. U.S. troops had participated, since Cambrai
in the fall of 1917, in most of the principal actions of the
Western Front, but in small units, as divisions, at most in
corps strength. Their presence, even in green units, was a
tremendous tonic to the Allies, a depressant to the Germans.
But the burdens of the big battles had been borne chiefly
by the British and French. The St.-Mihiel salient was almost
as old as the trench lines in the West. It protected Metz,
the Briey iron mines, and dominated two key railroad lines.
It was strongly seamed with field positions, though the
Germans—extended by other actions—did not have troops
enough to man them properly.

Pershing, insistent from the beginning upon the creation
of an American army, assembled some 550,000 Yankees from
all over France. The First U.S. Army (organized August 10),

under Pershing's command, numbered three U.S. corps, totaling fourteen American divisions, and four French divisions. Almost half the artillery pieces were manned by the French and all the guns and tanks were of French or British manufacture. The factories of America had not yet caught up with demands. The Allies far outnumbered the Germans, and as General Robert Bullard later noted, the German divisions were of poor quality—"young men and old, and Austro-Hungarians (35th Division).

". . . the St.-Mihiel battle was given an importance which posterity will not concede it." Bullard was right, for the Germans had already started the evacuation of the salient.

It was, nevertheless, a quick and satisfying success for the young but confident novitiates. The attack was supported by about 1,400 planes commanded by Colonel (later Brigadier General) William Mitchell, more than half of them flown by British and French pilots: the largest air force ever assembled. The converging attacks on the two faces of the salient preceded by a four-hour, one-million-round artillery bombardment were launched in dense fog on September 12 and quickly eliminated the bulge. Some 16,500 prisoners and 443 guns were captured in about four days and the American casualties—some seven thousand—were lighter than in other, harder fought actions. It was a small victory but a bracer; and Clemenceau and Poincaré and a host of others sent their congratulations.

Railroads were a major key to strategy in World War I. The German General Staff had won many of its greatest victories by masterly use of rail networks for troop movements and supplies.

In France, the German armies depended primarily upon the Mainz-Strasbourg, Coblenz-Virton, and Cologne-Maubeuge lines and the lateral Strasbourg-Metz-Thionville-Sedan-Mézières-Aulnoye-Maubeuge-Ghent-Bruges railroad for their supplies. The final battles of 1918 focused upon these rail lines; their control by the Allies would inevitably mean retreat and possibly disaster for the Germans.

Foch, like many of the Allied leaders, was prepared for

operations extending into 1919, but after the September successes he keyed his fall attacks to unremitting blows along much of the front against the groggy German armies.

"Tout le monde à la bataille!" was his battle cry.

Two main and roughly converging, or pincer, attacks were planned by the Americans and French from the Meuse-Argonne region, west of Verdun; and by the British and French from Lens to La Fère. The objectives were the rail junctions of Mézières and Sedan, and Aulnoye and Maubeuge. Other attacks were to be launched by King Albert of the Belgians in Flanders, with Belgian, British, and French support, and by French armies in the center.

At the end of September there were 39 U.S. divisions in France (29 took part in active combat; the rest were used as replacements or were just arriving), 102 French, 60 British, 12 Belgian, 2 Italian, and 2 Portuguese—a total of 217—opposing 193 German and 4 Austrian divisions, many of them under strength. But the huge American divisions were more than twice as large as the French, almost twice as large as the British, four times the size of some of the depleted German divisions. In terms of kilometers of front, the Americans held about one quarter of the total (157 kilometers on September 10; Belgians, 37 kilometers; British, 140; French, 388—a grand total of 722).[18] Six U.S. divisions served under British and French command in their offensive; the rest were concentrated in the U.S. First Army, and in a new Second Army, activated October 12, under General Bullard. (At this time, Pershing relinquished command of the First Army to General Hunter Liggett.)

The U.S. First Army, with the French Fourth Army (Gouraud) on its left flank, started the final drives of the war on September 26, with a three-corps offensive in the Meuse-Argonne—the greatest battle to that time of American arms. The army had been hastily concentrated after the St.-Mihiel offensive with the aid of careful plans, supervised by Colonel George C. Marshall, the assistant operations officer on the First Army staff. The assault made about three miles on the first day against light opposition, but soon the Americans were heavily engaged in the tangled maze of the Argonne forest, and around the stark heights of Montfaucon. By October 3, the Americans had bulled their way—with heavy casualties—across about one half of the Argonne forest, had taken Montfaucon, and their right flank rested south of Brieulles-sur-Meuse.

Meantime, the British launched a heavy assault on September 27 (with some forty-one divisions) in Picardy, between Péronne and Lens; King Albert of the Belgians attacked in the coastal lowlands on the twenty-eighth; and the British right wing and the French joined the massive attacks from Péronne to La Fère on the twenty-ninth. The British made about six miles on the first day—back to the gates of Cambrai, the rubbled scene of earlier battles. By October 5, the British, with the aid of one American corps, had broken through the Hindenburg Line.

Everywhere the fighting was fierce; the Germans retreated slowly, doggedly, delaying the Allies with machine-gun nests and skillful rear guards, protecting their lines of supply. But by September 28, Ludendorff, who tended to go to pieces under pressure, knew this was the end; he told Hindenburg an armistice should be concluded. Prince Max of Baden, appointed to make a peace, became Chancellor of Germany in early October, and on October 4, Germany and Austria requested President Wilson for an armistice on the basis of the "Fourteen Points."

But some of the fiercest fighting lay ahead. Everywhere from Verdun to the sea, the Allied line was moving forward now, for the first time in four long years. In the Argonne, from October 3 through the month the Yanks at heavy cost were making inching progress in the stygian gloom of the forest. Heads fell as Pershing replaced generals who had failed. The green divisions that had jumped off on September 26—there had been no time to move the veterans from St.-Mihiel—were relieved by more experienced troops. The Heights of the Meuse were cleared and by November 1, Granpré was in American hands—the Hindenburg Line was broken on a wide front—and the awful Argonne, with its

"Lost Battalion" (1st Battalion, 308th Infantry, 77th Division), was behind them. The heavy lock was smashed, the front unhinged, and from then until November 11, the American First Army (supported on its right flank by a French corps and the new U.S. Second Army) swept forward in great leaps. By the eleventh, the lateral rail line—Montmédy-Sedan-Mézières had been interdicted by American artillery; the 42nd (Rainbow) Division, Brigadier General Douglas MacArthur commanding, was in front of Sedan, and the French held Mézières.

In the North, the Belgians had taken Bruges and Ghent and were moving toward the Scheldt, the British held the rail junction of Maubeuge, the Canadians had cleared Mons, the Germans were having difficulty with supply, and the virus of defeat was spreading. But the fighting was still sporadically heavy, men were dying, when suddenly, at long, long last, the thing was finished.

The German collapse was a product of many factors: the huge cumulative losses from the war of attrition in the West; the bloody exactions of many fronts; the slow, inexorable economic pressure of the blockade; food shortages and war weariness; Bolshevist subversion and propaganda; liberal dissatisfaction with Germany's monarchical autocracy; and last but not least the impossible demands of a Napoleonic strategy of unlimited aims fashioned by a German general staff with delusions of grandeur and an arrogant concept of Germany *"über alles."* Germany had fought half the world, her armies had shown courage, discipline, and tactical skill unequaled, Ludendorff was a master tactician, Hutier a general of vision, Hoffmann a strategist, but the great and glaring weakness then—and later—was the impossible goal demanded of the German soldier, a goal evolved from the arrogant hauteur of a military-monarchical clique, and from the almost contemptuous underestimation of the enemy.

Bismarck's famous remark, "If an English army should ever set foot in Germany, it would be arrested," epitomized the Junker's attitude toward the "lesser breeds." Too many of the German General Staff, brilliant though limited soldiers that they were, had little feeling for the hearts of other men —a fatal defect in war or peace.

The final calendar of dissolution at the end of World War I compressed much agony and chaos into little time. The first appeal for an armistice to President Wilson in early October was followed by exchanges of notes and statements of conditions. But the vise was closing on Germany; she could set no conditions. The attempt to escape the inevitable ended in Ludendorff's resignation, under pressure, on October 27. Bulgaria had dropped out of the war in late September; Turkey signed an armistice on October 30; the Austrians on November 3. And in late October naval mutinies in the High Seas Fleet started to spread throughout the land. Socialist Friedrich Ebert became Chancellor on November 9; the Kaiser fled to Holland on the tenth, and at 5 A.M., November 11, in a railroad car in the Forest of Compiègne, where Hitler was to dance an obscene jig of joy another war later, a German delegation signed an armistice of defeat.

And so, at 11 A.M. November 11, 1918, the firing slowly died. Men came out of the trenches and foxholes from Switzerland to the sea and each in his own way celebrated victory or defeat—some in prayer, some in salutes, some simply in cadging cigarettes from the erstwhile foe.

Five thousand miles away, Lettow-Vorbeck, still playing hare to the British hound, had eluded capture or defeat for all of 1918. He had lived off the country, doubled Lake Nyasa, and was in northern Rhodesia when he learned of the Armistice. Eleven days after the fighting had ended in France, November 23, 1918, Lettow-Vorbeck surrendered unconquered, a minor military epic his claim to fame.

VII

TRUTH AND CONSEQUENCES

MAN MADE A DESERT and called it peace.

The Treaty of Versailles was not signed until late June, 1919, nine months after the birds began to sing again along the lunar landscape of the Western Front. The German representatives balked; some of the idealism of Wilson's Fourteen Points was clothed, in the event, in the ugly armor of power politics. But Germany was powerless to protest; the Armistice terms had seen to that.

By mid-December, 1918, Allied troops had closed up to the Rhine and occupied brigeheads across it—the British around Cologne, the Americans at Coblenz, the French at Mainz. All German submarines had been surrendered, interned, or scuttled. The German High Seas Fleet (eleven battleships, five battle cruisers, eight light cruisers, forty-nine destroyers[1]) lay helpless beneath the guns of the Grand Fleet at Scapa Flow (to be scuttled by its German crews in June, 1919). Artillery and machine guns by the thousands had been surrendered to the Allied armies. Balkiness was of no avail; a threat to march deeper into Germany sufficed.

A peace was imposed upon Europe: self-determination gone wild, some thought; idealism mated with pragmatism, others said; harsh, the Germans thought; too mild, the Allied peoples felt.

Like all histories of compromises built in blood, this one

—the Treaty of Versailles—was evanescent.

It encouraged the formation of democratic government in Germany, the Weimar Republic, but saddled it with guilt, reparations, and a host of troubles. It provided inspections and safeguards against the recrudescence of German militarism which the Allies failed to enforce. And on January 30, 1933, a brown-shirted dictator, Adolf Hitler—a courageous corporal in World War I—assumed more personal power than the Kaiser had ever had. It established out of the ashes of empire new nations—Poland and Czechoslovakia—but forty years afterward they were free and sovereign states in name only. It redrew the map of the Balkans, but the Balkans with their secret police, their spies and repression, their autocracy, changed in form but not in substance. It created, in the Polish corridor, separating Germany from East Prussia, an encouragement to irredentism, an incitement to rabble-rousers.

And when the United States repudiated its President and rejected the international organization the treaty established —the League of Nations—Europe was left to stew in its own juice. The withdrawal to a new kind of American isolationism, bred economically from boom times, psychologically from a slow reaction to the knowledge that the war had not made the world safe for democracy, was speeded in 1923 when American troops were withdrawn from the Rhineland. The British stayed until December, 1929, the French six months longer.

But the Treaty of Versailles, sometimes described as a treaty drawn by amateurs or schoolmasters, was an effect, a result, rather than a cause; it did not spawn the host of evils that followed in war's train. The war itself, unprecedented in scope, bloodshed, fury, and destruction, did this. The Four Horsemen of the Apocalypse rode across the world. The civil wars in Russia dragged on for more than two years, Bolshevism threatened Germany (December, 1918–February, 1919), appeared briefly in Central Europe as Béla Kun established a shortlived Communist government in Hungary (March-August, 1919), and

Joseph Pilsudski and his valiant Poles turned back the Red tide at the gates of Warsaw (August 14, 1920).

Disease swept the world; the great influenza epidemic of 1918-1919 killed 500,000 Americans, millions of others.[2] Typhus, smallpox, and the plagues flared amidst devastation. Famine stalked the rubble; pictures of babies with bloated stomachs and staring vacant eyes troubled the sleep of the well fed. An engineer named Herbert Hoover earned international fame by organizing famine relief and aid for Belgium, Russia, and other war-raddled nations. Greece, scavenging in Asia Minor, warred with the Turks for two long years until a general named Mustafa Kemal Atatürk, father of the New Turkey, slaughtered the invaders at Smyrna (September, 1922). Jewish immigration to Palestine and Arab factionalism and dissatisfaction with British and French policies increased tension in the Middle East and bloodshed —still unstanched—started. Germany's colonies in Africa became the spoils of conquest. In the western Pacific and the Far East, under Japan's rising sun, the doctrine of Asia for Asiatics sprouted its poisonous seed. And the consequences went on forever.

The statistics of Armageddon—staggering in terms of human and physical losses—provide the factual reasons for the long and tragic aftermath, the suffering still unended. In World War I, an earthquake shook the history of modern man. A total of at least 8,600,000 men in uniform were killed in battle or died of wounds or disease (some estimates exceed 10,000,000). At least 21,220,000 others were wounded. Russia, Austria, Germany, and France lost most heavily;[3] including prisoners and missing, their percentages of casualties ranged from 64.9 percent of the men mobilized in the case of Germany to 90 percent in the case of Austria.

The war cost about $338 billion; the United States started a national debt which it has never eliminated, and the costs keep marching on. Allied and neutral merchant ship losses totaled 12,850,000 tons (11,153,000 tons sunk by submarines).[4]

Hundreds of thousands were left homeless.

MILITARY CASUALTIES
(to Nearest Round Number).

Country	Killed and Died of Wounds or Disease	Wounded
Russia	1,700,000	4,950,000
Germany	1,773,000	4,216,000
France	1,385,000*	4,266,000
British Empire	908,400	2,090,200
Austria-Hungary	1,200,000	3,620,000
Italy	650,000	947,000
Turkey	325,000	400,000
Serbia and Montenegro	48,000	143,000
Belgium	14,000	44,700
Rumania	335,700*	120,000
Bulgaria	87,500	152,400
United States	116,516	234,428
Greece	5,000	21,000
Portugal	7,200	13,800

* Includes missing. All figures approximate only. (Civilian casualties caused by military action and by famine, disease, and the civil wars and disorders that followed the Great War are numbered in additional but uncounted millions.)

The war left many military lessons. Chief among these was the realization that modern war, in Clemenceau's famous phrase, was "too important to be left to the generals." World War I was a war of peoples: men and women, industries and farms, were harnessed to its service. It was, even more than the American Civil War, which was ultimately decided by the industrial superiority of the North, a war of the "big factories." The "big battalions" played their bloody role but the Russians, above all, epitomized the fate of a nation warring with inadequate industrial means. The United States discovered the meaning of the term "industrial mobilization"; big battalions were not enough; a million men could not spring to arms overnight. "Lead time"—preparation time—for conversion of factories from peace to war was needed.

The nation's plans were grandiose but its performance weak; 23,000 tanks were ordered from U.S. factories; 26 completed before war's end; only 130 artillery pieces out of 2,251 used by U.S. troops in battle were manufactured in the United States; of 8,850,000 rounds of artillery ammunition expended by U.S. forces in France, 208,327 were made in America.[5] The lesson of industrial mobilization was to serve the nation well in another war.

Both the British and the Allied machinery for the superior planning and guidance of war developed, under adversity, from chaos and unilateral efforts, to coordination and multinational aims. The generals of World War I—and the admirals—will probably not rank with the great captains of history, though some stand above the ruck. Allenby and Maude and Franchet d'Esperey; Haig, pedestrian, stubborn, and unperceptive but, in his few grand moments, grim in resolution in a testing time; Liman von Sanders, who did much with little; Ludendorff when at his best; Hoffmann; the Russian, Brusilov; Putnik the Serb; Hutier, master of the new tactics of infiltration; Joffre and Foch; Sir Roger Keyes, Hipper, and Admiral Sims; and, in smaller commands, Mustafa Kemal, the Turk, and Lettow-Vorbeck of East Africa—these and a few others deserve the accolade of exceptional remembrance.[6]

But the agonies of attrition and stalemate, epitomized by the Western Front, cannot fairly be blamed upon the generals. They lived in a period of warfare in which firepower, the machine gun and artillery, had far outpaced mobility. The land defense in World War I, based upon the machine gun, temporarily was stronger than the offense, though careful preparation and tactical ingenuity could mean—as the Germans showed again and again—less loss for the offense than for the defense. The Hutier tactics of infiltration which served, in sharply modified form, as the basis of German blitzkrieg of World War II, provided a key to breakthrough. But the armies of World War I were essentially horse drawn, and neither the plane nor the tank was developed sufficiently in numbers or capabilities to permit the exploitation of breakthrough.

On the sea, in the very era when the armored, big-gunned

battleship achieved its naval maturity, the submarine and the plane cast a long shadow across history. The immense importance of sea power was, perhaps, not fully recognized by the victors until the unrestricted submarine campaign of 1917 threatened Britain, though briefly, with defeat. The reverse of the coin—the fatal constriction of the blockade, slow, inexorable, and crushing upon Germany—was a primary factor in the Allied triumph; without it, the war could not have been won. And, too late for whole generations of British youth, England relearned the lessons of her maritime past: that naval wars, though expensive in matériel, are relatively cheap in human life. In comparison with the torrents of blood shed on the Western Front, the casualties at sea were minuscule: a total of 39,940 (including 33,527 dead) naval casualties for Britain, plus 14,661 killed in the merchant service. Germany suffered about 25,000 killed in the war at sea, 30,000 wounded, 12,000 prisoners.[7]

In the technical sense World War I provided a preview of the Pandora's box of evils that the linkage of science with industry in the service of war was to mean. The plane, particularly when used in what is now known as "strategic bombardment"—war upon the home front—was still a minor factor in 1914-1918. Forty-eight airship (dirigible) raids on Britain throughout the war cost 556 lives; 59 attacks by planes killed 857 Englishmen. About 720 German civilians were killed in comparable Allied air attacks.[8] Gas, used in great quantities, caused 91,198 deaths; 1,205,655 injured:[9] it is a far more potent weapon now than then. The tank and the plane and the truck and the missile and the nuclear-powered ship have mated mobility to the firepower unlimited that the atomic age now permits. Today, war is truly total: war of peoples, war of nations, war of big laboratories, big factories, and big battalions.

The political consequences of World War I still linger on. It may well have marked the beginning, in Spengler's gloomy words, of "the decline of the West"; certainly it stimulated the growth of world power centers in the Western Hemisphere (the United States and Canada) and in the

Far East (Japan) at the expense of Western Europe.

The bloodletting cost Britain dearly: she extended empire briefly but at the cost of the strength to hold it. It was Indian manpower (primarily) that conquered the Turks, but only for a brief interlude in the affairs of man did the British raj rule over the disrupted remnants of the ancient Turkish hegemony. With Indian independence after World War II, Britain was no longer powerful enough to maintain her position in the Middle East: a power vacuum was created, still struggling to be filled. Nor was Britain able to retain supremacy at sea; the United States and a potential rival, Japan, challenged, and ultimately surpassed, her.

And out of the seeds of revolution in Russia, there slowly grew to world power—aided by another global conflict—an empire far more mighty than any Britain had ever known.

For France, exhausted, devastated but still touched with the mystique of grandeur and glory, World War I was but a prelude to World War II, a chapter ended in tenuous victory which prefaced ultimate defeat.

For the United States, hurt but little in tangible terms, World War I meant the beginning of global power and influence, a central moment—no man may say how long—upon the ever-changing stage of history.

In a real sense the first Great War, and the second of 1939-1945, are chapters, episodes in a process still continuing—a huge convulsion in the affairs of man. Toynbee has called this twentieth century a "time of troubles"; the spark set at Sarajevo still flames across our world. Upon industrial revolution and political revolution have now been superimposed economic, social, and scientific revolution. And the end is not yet.

The days of kings and monarchies—save as vestigial figureheads of state—ended in World War I. But "the war to end war" did not end either war or tyranny; it did not bring the "brave new world"; dictators, demagogues, extremists—all bred from that fascinating mélange, the race of man—ruled, and still rule, the multitudes. Germany, defeated in 1918, soon forgot and opted once again for autocracy and conquest.

And once again—but at what bitter cost—went down to defeat.

For four years Germany fought and defied the five continents of the world by land and sea and air. The German Armies upheld her tottering confederates, intervened in every theatre with success, stood everywhere on conquered territory, and inflicted on their enemies more than twice the bloodshed they suffered themselves. To break their strength and science and curb their fury, it was necessary to bring all the greatest nations of mankind into the field against them. Overwhelming populations, unlimited resources, measureless sacrifice, the Sea Blockade, could not prevail for fifty months. Small states were trampled down in the struggle; a mighty Empire was battered into unrecognizable fragments; and nearly twenty million men perished or shed their blood before the sword was wrested from that terrible hand. Surely, Germans, for history it is enough![10]

NOTES

CHAPTER I. THE WAR IN PERSPECTIVE

1. Ivan S. Bloch, tr. by R. C. Long, *The Future of War, in Its Technical, Economic and Political Relations* (Boston: Ginn and Co., 1899). Translation of the last volume of the author's six-volume work on war, originally published in Europe in 1897. See, too, Quincy Wright's two-volume *A Study of War* (Chicago: University of Chicago Press, 1947).

2. I. S. Bloch's work led the Czar to suggest a peace conference—which became the Hague Conference of 1899. The quotations cited are from Gordon B. Turner, ed., *A History of Military Affairs in Western Society Since the Eighteenth Century* (prepared for the ROTC military history courses at Princeton University, Ann Arbor, Mich.: Edward Bros. Inc., 1952).

3. Turner, *ibid.*, vol. 1, p. 307.

4. Charles Seymour, ed., *Intimate Papers of Colonel House* (Boston: Houghton Mifflin Co., 1926), vol. 1, p. 249.

5. Ludwig Reiners, *The Lamps Went Out in Europe* (New York: Pantheon Books, 1955), p. 71. Chapter VII of this book presents a brilliant characterization of the Kaiser.

6. Reiners, *ibid.*

7. Col. T. Dodson Stamps, Col. Vincent J. Esposito, eds., *A Short Military History of World War I* (West Point, N. Y.: U. S. Military Academy, 1950), p. 5.

8. Stamps, *ibid.*, p. 9.

9. Stamps, *ibid.*, p. 10.

10. Stamps., *ibid.*, p. 9.

11. Pierce G. Fredericks, *The Great Adventure—America in the First*

World War (New York: E. P. Dutton and Co., Inc., 1960), p. 167. See also Brett and Douglas, *The Air Force Officer's Guide* (New York: McGraw-Hill Book Co., 1952), p. 26; John R. Cuneo, *The Air Weapon, 1914-16* (Harrisburg, Penna.: The Military Service Publishing Co., 1947).

12. The *Dreadnought* was completed in December, 1906, and represented the first of a new class of battleships that was to dominate the seven seas until World War II. She carried ten 12-inch guns, main belt armor of eleven inches, and was the first turbine-engined big ship in any navy. She was bunkered for both oil and coal. See Arthur J. Marder, *The Anatomy of British Sea Power* (New York: Alfred Knopf, 1940), chap. XXVII. See also, *Jane's Fighting Ships, 1914-1915-1916* (London: Sampson Low, Marston & Co. Ltd,).

13. Cyril Falls, *The Great War—1914-18* (New York: G. P. Putnam's Sons, 1959), p. 37. This is an excellent one-volume study, charitable in some ways to British generalship, but on the whole balanced and objective.

14. Stamps, *op. cit.*, p. 8.

15. Falls, *op. cit.*, p. 37.

16. Falls, *ibid.*, p. 38.

17. Grand Admiral Erich Raeder, *My Life* (Annapolis, Md.: U. S. Naval Institute, 1960), p. 59.

18. Commander Holloway H. Frost, U.S.N., *The Battle of Jutland* (Annapolis, Md.: U.S. Naval Institute, 1936), p. 516.

19. Reiners, *op. cit.*, p. 105.

20. Falls, *op. cit.*, p. 23.

21. Reiners, *op. cit.*, p. 110. Whether or not the Serbian government, *per se*, knew of the plot beforehand is still a matter of dispute between historians. Reiners thinks so; Falls doesn't. In any case, the Austrian government of the time, though it was able to trace the origin of the crime to Belgrade, could not pin it officially on the Serbian leaders.

22. House, *op. cit.*, vol. 1, p. 237.

23. James Cameron, *1914* (New York: Rinehart and Co., 1959), p. 84.

CHAPTER II. THE DIE IS CAST—1914

1. Gerhard Ritter, *The Schlieffen Plan* (New York: Frederick A. Praeger, 1958), p. 145.

2. Ritter, *ibid.* Schlieffen suggested one of the modifications.

3. Theodore Ropp, *War in the Western World* (Durham, N.C.: Duke University Press, 1959), p. 208.

4. Falls, *op. cit.*, p. 49.

5. Stamps, *op. cit.*, p. 42. Col. G. L. McEntee, *Military History of the World War,* (New York: Charles Scribner's Sons, 1937), p. 68; Ropp, *op. cit.*, p. 222. Ropp estimates the Allied forces on the western flank outnumbered the Germans fifty divisions to twenty-nine.

6. Stamps, *op. cit.*, p. 62.

7. Stamps, *ibid.*, p. 67. Stamps considers it "rather doubtful" that Foch actually sent this message, though it epitomized his spirit of resolution at the time. Colonel Stamps' reservation is justified. The famous message, though symbolic of Foch's determination, is not documented. Foch reported in writing: ". . . The situation is therefore excellent, and the attack directed against the Ninth Army appears to have been launched to cover the retreat of the German right wing." Foch may have amplified this orally, but it is more likely that legend magnified the facts.

8. Col. Vincent J. Esposito, chief ed., *The West Point Atlas of American Wars* (New York: Frederick A. Praeger, 1959), vol. II, Map 12.

9. Reiners, *op. cit.*, p. 174.

10. Winston S. Churchill, *The Unknown War* (New York: Charles Scribner's Sons, 1932), pp. 1, 2.

11. Esposito, *op. cit.*, says (Map 17) "despair and panic now seized the Eighth Army commander."

12. All Russian casualty figures are estimates only and these estimates vary widely. Then, as now, accurate Russian casualty reports were sparse; then, as now, grave-registration details were nonexistent. If a man did not return from the war he was assumed to be dead.

13. Stamps, *op. cit.*, p. 113.

14. Stamps, *ibid.*, p. 119.

15. McEntee, *op. cit.*, p. 133.

16. Frost, *op. cit.*; Falls, *op. cit.*

17. Sir J. S. Corbett (and Sir H. Newbolt), *British Official History—Naval Operations* (London: H. M. Stationery Office, 1921), vol. I, pp. 345-357.

18. Corbett, *ibid.*, vol. I, chap. XXIX.

CHAPTER III. THE GIANTS ARE LOCKED—1915

1. Falls, *op. cit.*: p. 118.

2. McEntee *op. cit.*, pp. 178-179.

3. Col. Alden H. Waitt, *Gas Warfare* (New York: Duell, Sloan and Pearce, 1942), p. 17.

4. John R. Cuneo, *The Air Weapon 1914-16, Vol. II of Winged Mars* (Harrisburg: The Military Service Publishing Co., 1947), p. 167.

5. Frederick Oughton, *The Aces* (New York: G. P. Putnam's Sons, 1960).

6. McEntee, *op. cit.*, p. 224.

7. Ropp, *op. cit.*, p. 235.

8. Alan Moorehead, *Gallipoli* (New York: Harper & Brothers, 1956), p. 40.

9. Moorehead, *ibid.*, p. 112.

10. Ropp, *op. cit.*, p. 235, and Moorehead, *op. cit.*, p. 361.

11. John Clinton Adams, *Flight in Winter* (Princeton: Princeton University Press, 1942).

12. H. W. Wilson, *Battleships in Action* (Boston: Little, Brown and Co., 1926) vol. II, p. 97.

13. Lt. Gen. Nicholas N. Golovine, *The Russian Army in the World War* (New Haven: Yale University Press, 1931), p. 222. Golovine's figures, however, are purely estimates and considerably in excess of others.

CHAPTER IV. STRUGGLE OF ATTRITION—1916

1. Lt. Col. Paul W. Thompson, "Sevastopol and Verdun" (Washington: *Infantry Journal*, Jan., 1943), pp. 9-17. The actual effects upon the forts were negligible; see Vivian Rowe, *The Great Wall of France* (New York: G. P. Putnam's Sons, 1961), p. 22.

2. Thompson, *ibid*.

3. McEntee, *op. cit.*, p. 275.

4. Falls, *op. cit.*, p. 190.

5. McEntee, *op. cit.*, p. 291

6. B. H. Liddell Hart, *The Tanks—A History of the Royal Tank Regiment* (New York: Frederick A. Praeger, 1959), vol. 1, p. 47.

7. Frost, *op. cit.*, pp. 507-509, 539-542. See also H. W. Wilson, *Battleships in Action*, *op. cit.*, and Hanson W. Baldwin, *Sea Fights and Shipwrecks* (Garden City: Hanover House, 1955), pp. 267-286.

8. E. B. Potter, ed., Fleet Admiral Chester W. Nimitz, assoc. ed., *Sea Power—A Naval History* (Englewood Cliffs, New Jersey: Prentice-Hall, 1960), p. 459.

9. Lt. Col. Arnold T. Wilson, *Loyalties, Mesopotamia, 1914-1917* (London: Oxford University Press, 1930), pp. 91-100.

10. The name "Lenin," though world famous, was a pseudonym or pen name. Lenin's actual name was Vladimir Ilyich Ulyanov. The "N" was a prefix, which stood for nothing. He also used the pseudonyms "Tulin" and "Ilin," but he has come to be known to history as Vladimir Ilyich Lenin.

CHAPTER V. THE FATEFUL YEAR—1917

1. *Statistics of the Military Effort of the British Empire During the Great War* (London: His Majesty's Stationery Office, 1922), p. 487.

2. McEntee, *op. cit.*, p. 351 quoted.

3. *Statistics*, *op. cit.*, p. 640.

4. McEntee, *op. cit.*, p. 358.

5. David Lloyd George, *War Memoirs* (Boston: Little, Brown and Co., 1934), vol. IV, pp. 338, 339.

6. George Dock, Jr., Letter to the author. Malinovsky, then eighteen years old, is described as a corporal in Walter Kerr, *The Russian Army* (New York: Alfred A. Knopf, 1944), pp. 21, 22.

7. Ropp, *op. cit.*, p. 235.

8. Alan Moorehead, *Gallipoli* (New York: Harper & Brothers, 1956), p. 40.

9. Moorehead, *ibid.*, p. 112.

10. Ropp, *op. cit.*, p. 235, and Moorehead, *op. cit.*, p. 361.

11. John Clinton Adams, *Flight in Winter* (Princeton: Princeton University Press, 1942).

12. H. W. Wilson, *Battleships in Action* (Boston: Little, Brown and Co., 1926) vol. II, p. 97.

13. Lt. Gen. Nicholas N. Golovine, *The Russian Army in the World War* (New Haven: Yale University Press, 1931), p. 222. Golovine's cavalry could be used as an arm of exploitation still persisted even at Cambrai.

12. George F. Kennan, *Russia Leaves the War* (Princeton: Princeton University Press, 1956), pp. 8-9.

13. Georg von Rauch, *A History of Soviet Russia* (New York: Frederick A. Praeger, 1957), pp. 39 ff.

14. Rauch, *op. cit.*, p. 60, quoted from Leon Trotsky, *The History of the Russian Revolution* (New York; 1936), vol. III, p. 311.

15. Kennan, *op. cit.*, p. 228.

16. H. C. Peterson, *Propaganda for War* (Norman, Oklahoma: University of Oklahoma Press, 1939).

17. Pierce G. Fredericks, *The Great Adventure* (New York: E. P. Dutton and Co., Inc., 1960), pp. 29-30.

18. Elting E. Morison, *Admiral Sims and the Modern American Navy* (Boston: Houghton Mifflin Co., 1942), p. 342.

19. Rear Admiral William Sowden Sims, U.S.N., *The Victory at Sea* (New York: Doubleday, Page and Co., 1920), p. 9.

20. Morison, *op. cit.*, p. 343.

21. Sims, *op. cit.*, p. 64.

22. Wilson, *op. cit.*, vol. II, pp. 221-231.

23. Fredericks, *op. cit.*, p. 147.

24. McEntee, *op. cit.*, p. 451.

25. Falls, *op. cit.*, p. 328.

26. Maj. Gen. J. F. C. Fuller, *The Decisive Battles of the Western World* (London: Eyre and Spottiswoode, 1956), vol. III, p. 269.

27. Lynn Montross, *War Through the Ages* (New York: Harper & Brothers, 1944), p. 740.

CHAPTER VI. EXHAUSTION AND VICTORY—1918

1. Rauch, *op. cit.*, p. 76.

2. McEntee, *op. cit.*, p. 463; and Falls, *op. cit.*, pp. 288, 331.

3. E. M. Halliday, *The Ignorant Armies* (New York: Harper & Brothers, 1960).

4. Wilson, *op. cit.*, p. 211.

5. Baldwin, *op. cit.*, pp. 121-133.

6. Sims, *op. cit.*, p. 366.

7. *Ibid.*, p. 340.

8. Wilson, *op. cit.*, p. 216.

9. *Ibid.*, p. 215.

10. Figures for air strengths of the combatants vary widely. See Ayres, *op. cit.*, chap. VII and p. 143; H. A. Jones, *The War in the Air* (Oxford: Clarendon Press, 1937), vol. VII, Appendix XL, and Fredericks, *op. cit.*, chap. VII.

11. Falls, *op. cit.*, p. 393.

12. *West Point Atlas of American Wars, op. cit.,* Map 50.

13. McEntee, *op. cit.*, p. 564.

14. Falls, *op. cit.*, p. 331.

15. Colonel Leonard P. Ayres, *The War with Germany—A Statistical Summary* (Washington: Government Printing Office, 1919), pp. 14, 15, 33; and McEntee, *op. cit.*, pp. 496-497.

16. Ayres, *op. cit.*, pp. 33, 37.

17. McEntee, *op. cit.*, p. 506.

18. Falls, *op. cit.*, p. 408; and Ayres, chap. VIII.

CHAPTER VII. TRUTH AND CONSEQUENCES

1. Wilson, *op. cit.*, pp. 323-324. Paul Schubert, Langhorne Gibson, *Death of a Fleet* (New York: Coward-McCann, Inc., 1932).

2. H. H. Hockling, *The Great Epidemic* (Boston: Little, Brown & Co., 1961), p. 3.

3. Casualty statistics are estimates derived from Ayres, *op. cit.*, chap. IX; *Statistics of the British Empire, op. cit.*, p. 352; Falls, *op. cit.*, p. 424; Reiners, *op. cit.*, p. 295; Golovine, *op. cit.*, pp. 94, 98; and many others.

4. Wilson, *op. cit.*, pp. 232-233.

5. Ayres, *op. cit.*, chaps. V, VI; Cols. George C. Reinhardt, William R. Kintner, *The Haphazard Years* (Garden City, N.Y.: Doubleday and Co., 1961), chap. III.

6. Pershing, who proved to be a fine organizer, disciplinarian, and administrator, trained the AEF well, though some of his tactical ideas were obsolescent. But he had no real chance to prove his generalship.

7. Wilson, *op. cit.*, p. 324.

8. *Statistics of the British Empire, op. cit.*, p. 674.

9. Lt. Col. A. M. Prentiss, *Chemicals in War* (New York: McGraw-Hill Book Co., 1937), p. 653.

10. Winston S. Churchill, *The World Crisis* (New York: Charles Scribner's Sons, 1927), vol. II, pp. 275, 276.

SELECTED BIBLIOGRAPHY

CAUSES AND ORIGINS

Sidney Bradshaw Fay, *The Origins of the World War* (N. Y.: The Macmillan Co., 1939)

Ludwig Reiners, *The Lamps Went Out in Europe* (N. Y.: Pantheon Books, 1955)

Joachim Remak, *Sarajevo—The Story of a Political Murder* (N. Y.: Criterion, 1959)

MAPS

Colonel Vincent J. Esposito, chief ed., *The West Point Atlas of American Wars* (N. Y.: Frederick A. Praeger, 1959)

OFFICIAL HISTORIES

U. S. Army in the World War, 1917-19 (Washington: Historical Division, Department of the Army, vol. 1-17, 1948)

BRITISH OFFICIAL HISTORIES

Military Operations (London: MacMillan and Co., 1922-1948, vol. 1-28)

Naval Operations (London: Longmans, Green, 1920-1931, vol. 1-5)

The War in the Air (Oxford, Clarendon Press, 1922-1937, vol. 1-7)

GENERAL HISTORIES

Cyril Falls, *The Great War, 1914-1918* (N. Y.: G. P. Putnam's Sons, 1959)

Major General J. F. C. Fuller, *The Decisive Battles of the Western World* (London: Eyre and Spottiswoode, 1956)

B. H. Liddell Hart, *A History of the World War, 1914-18* (London: Faber and Faber, 1934)

Colonel G. L. McEntee, *Military History of the World War*, with 456 maps and diagrams (N. Y.: Charles Scribner's Sons, 1937)

Theodore Ropp, *War in the Western World* (Durham, N.C.: Duke University Press, 1959)

Colonel T. Dodson Stamps, Colonel Vincent J. Esposito, eds., *A Short Military History of World War I* (West Point, N.Y.: U.S. Military Academy, 1950)

MEMOIRS

Winston S. Churchill, *The World Crisis* (N.Y.: Charles Scribner's Sons, 1920)

David Lloyd George, *War Memoirs* (Boston: Little, Brown and Co., 1934)

Rear Admiral William S. Sims, *The Victory at Sea* (N.Y.: Doubleday, Page and Co., 1920)

CAMPAIGNS: THE EASTERN FRONT

Winston S. Churchill, *The Unknown War* (N.Y.: Charles Scribner's Sons, 1932)

Lieutenant General Nicholas N. Golovine, *The Russian Army in the World War* (New Haven: Yale University Press, 1931)

George F. Kennan, *Russia Leaves the War* (Princeton: Princeton University Press, 1956)

CAMPAIGNS: THE WAR AT SEA

Commander Holloway H. Frost, *The Battle of Jutland* (Annapolis: U.S. Naval Institute, 1936)

E. B. Potter, Fleet Admiral Chester W. Nimitz, eds., *Sea Power—A Naval History* (Englewood Cliffs, N.J.: Prentice-Hall, 1960)

H. W. Wilson, *Battleships in Action* (Boston: Little, Brown and Co., 1926)

CAMPAIGNS: THE WAR IN THE AIR

John R. Cuneo, *The Air Weapon, 1914-16* (Harrisburg, Pa.: The Military Service Publishing Co., 1947)

Frederick Oughton, *The Aces* (N.Y.: G. P. Putnam's Sons, 1960)

CAMPAIGNS: THE DARDANELLES

Alan Moorehead, *Gallipoli* (N.Y.: Harper & Brothers, 1956)

CAMPAIGNS: THE WESTERN FRONT

Leon Wolff, *In Flanders Fields: The 1917 Campaign* (N.Y.: The Viking Press, 1958)

CAMPAIGNS: THE SERBIAN RETREAT

John Clinton Adams, *Flight in Winter* (Princeton: Princeton University Press, 1942)

CAMPAIGNS: MESOPOTAMIA

Lieutenant Colonel Arnold T. Wilson, *Loyalties—Mesopotamia* (Oxford: Oxford University Press, 1930)

WEAPONS: TANKS

B. H. Liddell Hart, *The Tanks—A History of the Royal Tank Regiment* (N.Y.: Frederick A. Praeger, 1959)
Richard M. Ogorkiewicz, *Armor—A History of Mechanized Forces* (N.Y.: Frederick A. Praeger, 1960)

WEAPONS: GAS

Major General Charles Howard Foulkes, *"Gas!"—The Story of the Special Brigade* (Edinburgh: Blackwood and Sons, 1934)
James Kendall, *Breathe Freely!—The Truth About Poison Gas* (N.Y.: Appleton-Century Crofts, 1938)
Lieutenant Colonel A. M. Prentiss, *Chemicals in War* (N.Y.: McGraw-Hill Book Co., 1937)
Colonel Alden H. Waitt, *Gas Warfare* (N.Y.: Duell, Sloan and Pearce, 1942)

WEAPONS: AIRSHIPS

Ernst A. Lehmann and Howard Mingos, *The Zeppelins* (N.Y.: J. H. Sears and Co., 1927)

PROPAGANDA

H. C. Peterson, *Propaganda for War* (Norman, Okla.: University of Oklahoma Press, 1939)

STATISTICS

Colonel Leonard P. Ayres, *The War with Germany—A Statistical Summary* (Washington: U.S. Government Printing Office, 1919)

Marvin Kriedbirg, Lt. Merton Henry, *The History of Mobilization in the U.S. Army, 1775-1945* (Washington: U.S. Government Printing Office, Department of Army Pamphlet 20-212, 1948)

Statistics of the Military Effort of the British Empire During the Great War (London: His Majesty's Stationery Office, 1922)

INDEX